Stress-Free
Discipline

Stress-Free Discipline

Simple Strategies for Handling Common Behavior Problems

Sara Au

Peter L. Stavinoha, Ph.D.

AMACOM

American Management Association
New York • Atlanta • Brussels • Chicago • Mexico City
San Francisco • Shanghai • Tokyo • Toronto • Washington, D. C.

Bulk discounts available. For details visit:
www.amacombooks.org/go/specialsales
Or contact special sales:
Phone: 800-250-5308
Email: specialsls@amanet.org
View all the AMACOM titles at: www.amacombooks.org
American Management Association: www.amanet.org

This publication is designed to provide accurate and authoritative information in regard to the subject matter covered. It is sold with the understanding that the publisher is not engaged in rendering legal, accounting, or other professional service. If legal advice or other expert assistance is required, the services of a competent professional person should be sought.

Library of Congress Cataloging-in-Publication Data

Au, Sara.
  Stress-free discipline : simple strategies for handling common behavior problems / Sara Au and Peter L. Stavinoha, Ph.D.
     pages cm
  Includes bibliographical references and index.
  ISBN 978-0-8144-4909-7 (pbk.) — ISBN 0-8144-4909-3 (pbk.) — ISBN 978-0-8144-4910-3 (ebook) — ISBN 0-8144-4910-7 (ebook) 1. Discipline of children. 2. Parenting. I. Stavinoha, Peter L. II. Title.
  HQ770.4.A92 2015
  649'.64—dc23   2014028025

About AMA
American Management Association (www.amanet.org) is a world leader in talent development, advancing the skills of individuals to drive business success. Our mission is to support the goals of individuals and organizations through a complete range of products and services, including classroom and virtual seminars, webcasts, webinars, podcasts, conferences, corporate and government solutions, business books, and research. AMA's approach to improving performance combines experiential learning—learning through doing—with opportunities for ongoing professional growth at every step of one's career journey.

Printing number

10 9 8 7 6 5 4 3 2 1

Contents

PART II
Dealing with Areas of Common Difficulty

PART III
Develop Positive Characteristics

PART IV
Recognize Red Flags

Introduction and Philosophy

antrums! Homework! Mealtime! Bedtime! And then there's the attitude starting. . . .

If you're parenting a child, you're under a lot of stress, and that stress is most pronounced when you're dealing with a behavioral problem. Kids are also under a *lot* more stress today, so it's no wonder that clashes are frequent and that common ground seems rare. But it doesn't have to be that way. You can use discipline to cultivate a positive relationship with your child and alleviate many behavioral issues.

Start by taking a moment to think about what the term *discipline* means to you. If you're like many people, you may interpret it as synonymous with *punishment*. Within the pages of *Stress-Free Discipline*, we'll broaden that interpretation.

Discipline is counseling, consoling, coaching, ignoring, practicing, praising, and sometimes punishing, according to the values of your family. Discipline is an investment in your child's future, not just the correction of the behavior in front of you at any given moment. Discipline is shaping your child's behavior toward the outcome you want. More than anything, *discipline is education*.

It's essential for you to understand that discipline is *not* simply punishment—that punishment is simply *one* method of discipline. This book offers a whole new repertoire of strategies on a par with punishment to put in your parenting arsenal, including positive reinforcement, role-modeling, and restitution. We will teach you to learn from each experience handling a behavioral situation with your child and to self-correct your approach. Additionally, you need to examine your own life choices, such as how busy you are, your time and resources, as well as your own relationships and self-care, to see how they fit in with your child's behavior.

Children need to feel loved by the person or persons parenting them and to know their value in the world. But love is not the same thing as permissiveness. Parental love means saying *no* to your child at times when it's in her best interest. Love is inextricably intertwined with discipline. Taken together, love and discipline form the most solid foundation for life that can be provided to a child.

> *Love is inextricably intertwined with discipline.*

Picture yourself as a gardener just starting to organize and cultivate an overgrown backyard. You first must make a plan for what you're going to plant and where you're going to plant it. You then have to start weeding, being careful to identify what is growing before you decide to pull it out or keep it. After that, you need to till the soil, turn it over with fertilizer, and, finally, plant the seeds. But planting is just the beginning. You've also got to water the garden and nurture its growth. And, of course, you have to keep feeding, watering, and monitoring your plants on a regular schedule.

We'll be doing all that with you as you learn how to tend the garden that is your family. Just as different plants need different kinds of care, soil, and sunlight, each of your children will need his or her own version of your discipline approach.

An understanding of your child's motivations will help you weed out some bad behaviors from his garden and till the soil for the new seeds. Being an attentive parent is like a regular watering schedule: It nourishes your child. Before long, seedlings will mature into young plants, stretching green leaves up into the sky to capture as much sunlight as possible and drilling roots to anchor themselves tightly to that which fortifies them. Love and discipline root your child deeply, so he grows straight and strong, and doesn't bow to negative influences later in life. Good disciplinary methods will help your child blossom and grow into a strong, healthy, thriving, beautiful individual.

Getting your child from where she is today to where you want her to be as an adult is what parenting is all about, so before we get into tips, tactics, and psychological insight, let's start with an affirmation for you:

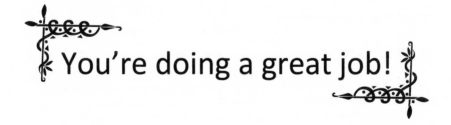

You're doing a great job!

Now, we authors are parents, too, and we know it's not that easy to hold onto a positive thought like this when you're in the thick of a difficult situation. Without a crystal ball, it's really hard to know if what you're doing is right, especially when every day seems to bring another problem. That's really the crux of why we wanted to write *Stress-Free Discipline*: to explain *why* kids behave the way they do and help you connect the context of those *why*s to your response to their behavior. Once you understand the *why*, you can figure out how to make some changes.

Positive behavior is a skill that all children have to acquire, just like potty training, learning how to pump their legs on the swings, and saying the alphabet. Children are not born knowing all the rules, boundaries, and manners of good behavior. They don't know how to peacefully resolve conflicts with siblings and peers, how to settle down for bed, or that certain words are off limits in our society. Those are things that have to be specifically taught, cultivated, and nurtured.

Stress-Free Discipline begins by explaining that behavior is communication. Part I consists of an explanation of the ABCs of behavior, which allow you to decode what your child is trying to tell you when he or she acts out. Whether you're about to embark on this leg of your parenting journey and are looking to smooth the path ahead, or if you're already down the road, wondering if you took a wrong turn, our 16 Universal Strategies will help you avoid or defuse difficult situations, stop the bad behavior, and forge a positive direction forward with your child.

Part II offers an in-depth look at some of the most common situations in which your child may exhibit behavioral challenges: tantrums, homework, mealtime, bedtime, and attitudes. Complete with examples and even sample scripts you can use with your child, this section provides response tactics that align with the basic tenets of child development and help you

> *Behavior is communication.*

handle every problem that arises in a calm, stress-free, confident manner.

Part III is all about proactive steps you can take to develop the kinds of positive characteristics in your child that will help her grow into a happy, productive, and fulfilled adult with whom you continue to have a loving relationship. From the essentials of a healthy social network to instilling a sense of resilience and grit, this discussion will benefit your entire family.

Finally, in Part IV, we'll take you through the kinds of red flags that may signal your child is under too much stress and that you might need to consider seeking professional help. There's no rhyme or reason to how any individual will respond to a particularly stressful situation, but we'll go through some common scenarios and give you guidance in making a decision.

By investing substantial time and strategic effort now, you can set positive habits and behaviors that show up naturally in your child when he is older. Discipline is very much a long-term process: It's never easy, and it can be ex-

Discipline is very much a long-term process.

hausting to keep up with it all, but it pays off when you see the wonderful person your child is growing into with your guidance. Keeping a long-term perspective is key to removing the stress you may feel while parenting. Understanding the reasons behind your child's behavior, and being able to react appropriately, will further reduce strain. This is the *Stress-Free Discipline* philosophy.

PART I

Understand Discipline from the Inside Out

1

Decode Your Child's Behavior

A parent's job is never easy, or over! Discipline may seem an insurmountable challenge. That's especially true if you're reading this book in reaction to your child's continued bad behavior, which has finally pushed you, or your partner, to a breaking point. But starting now, we want you to clear your mind of those troubles. We know it's hard, but you're going to start new with a blank slate and a fresh outlook.

You're probably wondering, "Okay, Dr. Pete and Sara—how exactly do we do that?"

First, understand that parenting is not simply black and white, right or wrong. There's no set of rules that say we all have to do things the same way. You'll find you've made mistakes, like all of us do, but don't let them make you feel paralyzed, or guilty, or inadequate. This is a learning curve for you and your child, and you're both more resilient than you may think.

Second, we want you to know these two essential truths about child behavior:

1. Most of what you're seeing is probably just normal behavior for a child.
2. It may feel like it sometimes, but your children are not *intentionally* trying to drive you crazy.

Sometimes, driving you crazy is just a by-product of their learning. Take a deep breath in . . . and out.

Knowledge is always a great de-stressor, because it more fully informs your decision making and reactions, which for so many of us is where that angst lives. That's never as true as in parenting. Learning how something works is necessary to be able to correct problems when they arise, as well as to prevent them before they arise.

Understanding the normal functioning of a child's mind helps us recognize when something *really* is wrong, as opposed to the typical challenges that we should expect. Child behavior involves an awful lot of trial and error. You can't freak out if something happens just a few times. It may simply be your child testing his or her boundaries, trying to find the right behavioral path in a world where things are not always predictable.

In this chapter, we take you through normal childhood behaviors. We also help you develop an awareness of the kinds of influences that lead to both good and bad behaviors. Additionally, we explain how you can understand your child's motives, and examine behavior as communication. You'll learn to decode your child's behavior in order to figure out how to shape it.

Knowledge is always a great de-stressor.

Most Problem Behavior Is Normal

What exactly is normal child behavior? *Normal* is a very broad term when applied to child behavior. The fact is that most kids, by definition, are normal, which means that most child behavior is normal, or at least explainable—even the stuff parents don't like. Remember that our definition of discipline is education. This book will help you take those behaviors that are normal, but undesirable, and shape them into the kinds of behaviors you want to encourage.

> *Most behaviors that we consider inappropriate are simply part of child development.*

Many behaviors that we consider inappropriate are simply part of child development. Take tantrums, for example. Little kids have tantrums sometimes as a method by which to express frustration, and they may hit or kick others as an attempt to get their way or may say things out of anger that are very hurtful. These are actually developmentally appropriate behaviors for children and are a part of growing up. Kids don't yet know all the rules, and they don't yet understand how their behavior may affect others. They test limits and boundaries (and parents' patience) as a natural part of the development process. Children are learning how far is too far and what reactions they can trigger, while simultaneously trying to satisfy their needs and wants and learning to express emotions in an acceptable manner.

That's not to say that you allow the hitting, kicking, or mean language to go unchecked, but even if some of these behaviors are repeated, please be reassured this is *normal* behavior. None of this reflects on your child's innate goodness or your ability to be a good parent. If you can keep that perspective, you'll do

You can affect behavior by controlling antecedents and using consequences.

wonders for your stress level! (But if you *are* experiencing severe behavioral issues that you believe may go beyond normal and beyond your ability to manage or understand them, in Chapter 11 we discuss what goes into deciding to seek professional help.)

Before you can shape behavior, you need to understand behavior in general. When psychologists analyze a behavior, they think in terms of the *ABC* formula for behavior management: *Antecedent, Behavior, Consequence*. While this may seem a little technical, stick with us because throughout this book we will show you how you can affect behavior by controlling antecedents and using consequences in a wide variety of ways. First, though, we need to go through these terms and have a common vocabulary.

For our purposes, the *antecedent* is the buildup of events, the contributing factors, and sometimes the triggers that lead to the child's behavior. The *behavior* is the response the child has in reaction to it. The *consequence* is what happens after the behavior that makes it more or less likely the behavior will occur again. A parent's reaction to the child after the behavior can be one powerful consequence, as can punishments. However, there are many other potential consequences (intended and not) that can influence whether the behavior is repeated.

All behavior, positive and negative, follows the ABC pattern. The situations of each component are what vary widely, from person to person and circumstance to circumstance. Children are still learning the most basic of appropriate responses to the world that touches them, so they very often have to learn by watching your reactions, or by trial and error.

The clues to your child's motivations for his behavior, and ultimately the prudent actions that you can take, lie within the context of this formula. These are the keys to unlocking your family's stress-free discipline plan.

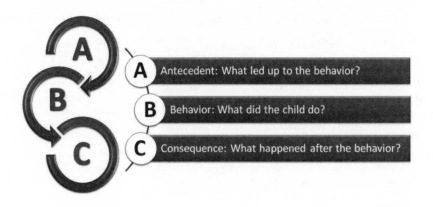

A — Antecedent: What led up to the behavior?

B — Behavior: What did the child do?

C — Consequence: What happened after the behavior?

In its most simplified form, parents should reflect on ABC by asking two questions in the context of a particular situation:

1. Did the events that happened *before the behavior* make it *more* likely or *less* likely that my child would behave in a manner that I did not want? (Antecedent)
2. Did what happened *after the behavior* make it *more* likely or *less* likely that my child will exhibit that behavior in the future? (Consequence)

At first, asking yourself these questions may feel unnatural or unwieldy to consider during the heat of the moment. But as you reflect afterward, you'll likely start seeing patterns of behavior in your child, and will be able to help shape his or her behavior in more effective ways. Eventually, asking yourself these questions will become second nature, but it's also possible you'll have fewer of those moments with which to contend.

Here's an example of the ABCs of child behavior as seen from three simple scenarios that each begin the same way.

Scenario One: Mya is happily playing with a friend in the play-room. The two have been getting along pretty well for an hour when all of a sudden Mya grabs a toy away from her friend. The friend screams in indignation, and Mom intervenes and makes Mya give the toy back.

> *Antecedent.* There are two girls playing for an hour, and one toy in particular seems to be most popular with them both.
>
> *Behavior.* Mya grabs the toy away.
>
> *Consequence.* The parent intervenes, and Mya has to give the toy back. Mya learns that she'll have to give something back if she grabs it away, which makes it *less* likely that she'll repeat this behavior.

Scenario Two: Let's look at the same situation with a little twist. After Mya grabs the toy, what if the other child whimpers but doesn't react in any larger way and the parents don't notice the tiff?

> *Antecedent.* Still the same.
>
> *Behavior.* Still the same.
>
> *Consequence.* Mya learns that grabbing gets her what she wants, which reinforces her behavior and makes it *more* likely she's going to do it again.

Scenario Three: Here's another twist: The children are playing and Mya's mother says, "Mya, you're doing such a great job sharing with your friend. High five, sweetie!"

Antecedent. Still the same.

Behavior. The toys are shared! The grab never happens because the parent has just reinforced the idea of sharing in Mya's mind.

Consequence. Mya learns that she gets praise from her mom when she shares, which makes it *more* likely that she'll share again at the next playdate.

As we said, these are very simple scenarios, and we all know that praising your child once won't teach her to share. These three examples were aimed at giving you an obvious blueprint to the ABCs of behavior so you can identify each point in the cycle and see where you can start to shape behavior. There are a great many nuanced tactics that go into shaping behavior, and we take you through them for the most common stress points in the next few chapters.

Because parents can control antecedents and consequences to some extent, those are primary methods of dealing with behavior. A lot of the work of parenting involves manipulating A and C in order to impact B.

Most of us understand the concept that if we give our child a consequence, we can manage behavior. Punish bad behavior to make it stop. (So you know, punishments don't always work, and, if they do, they often have merely short-term benefits; but more on this in the Universal Strategies in Chapter 2.) We've all used that word *consequences* countless times with our kids, and probably we heard it ourselves ad nauseam growing up:

"Be careful, or you'll have to face the consequences!"
"Listen up, or there will be consequences!"

But let's turn that on its end: Consequences do not simply consist of punishments. Praise is also a consequence. In fact, *any-*

Identify the ABCs

Think back to the most recent behavioral issue in your family. Can you identify the antecedent, behavior, and consequence?

Antecedent: _____

_____

_____

_____

Behavior: _____

_____

_____

_____

Consequence: _____

_____

_____

_____

How could you have reframed this situation to positively affect your child's behavior? Could you have avoided some of the contributing factors or triggers that served as antecedents? What if you chose a different consequence? Would that have made it more or less likely the behavior will repeat? Try making these changes the next time this situation crops up.

thing that happens *after* a behavior that impacts the likelihood of the behavior occurring again is considered a consequence.

Here's an example:

Antecedent: Jake and his dad take a boys' day to go to a baseball game. It's a last-minute treat because someone in Dad's office had two tickets he couldn't use. They'd been meaning to go all season but just hadn't got there until today.

Behavior: After they get home from the game, Jake's dad starts doing a few chores to get ready for the next day. As he's taking out the trash, he sees Jake come in and start to help by sorting the recyclables into the right bins and then dragging the bins out to the curb, where he sees his dad put them each week.

Consequence: Jake's dad thanks him for helping, and then later in the kitchen Jake overhears him bragging to his mom about how nice and responsible Jake was in helping. Jake loves feeling responsible, and was proud when he heard his dad saying such nice things about him to his mom. This makes it more likely that he will repeat the helpful behavior in the future. Jake's mom and dad realize that more one-on-one time is likely to promote positive behavior and that sincere praise and acknowledgment further encourage that type of behavior.

We're going to take a more nuanced look at the concept of punishing bad behavior and praising good behavior as we go through this book. Consequences can be highly effective, and since it's what most of us currently use, we go through the concept in more detail in Chapter 2. Often, we parents fall back on negative consequences when we find ourselves in uncharted territory, discipline-wise, and that's okay. Sometimes it's most appropriate. Sometimes it gets your child's attention more quickly.

> *Positive reinforcements and negative consequences are a powerful combination.*

But giving a negative consequence is just the beginning, and it shouldn't be your only tool. If it has been thus far, that may be the cause of some of your parental frustration. Avoiding problematic triggers, interrupting contributing factors, and using praise can shape your child's behavior just as effectively as using a negative consequence. Taken together, positive reinforcements and negative consequences are a powerful combination of parenting tools.

Know this: Your child may not even be making a choice when it comes to bad behaviors. We adults think about choosing our actions, but our children may not yet be at that stage developmentally where any behavior is truly a conscious choice. Often, they are just acting on impulse, some more so than others.

Keeping vigilant about the contributing factors that lead to an undesirable behavior may sometimes be more effective (not to mention avoiding the combat that sometimes goes hand-in-hand with negative consequences). For example, by paying attention to the trigger in a number of meltdowns, you may start to see a pattern: that your child is not likely to follow directions well when she's tired and grumpy.

It seems pretty obvious as you read that paragraph, right? Often, again in the heat of the moment, it's easy to overlook the realities of hunger and tiredness as connected to bad behavior. We just see a child who isn't following directions. But when fewer or simpler directions are given to a tired and grumpy kid, we see fewer problems. Save the other directions until he or she is alert and awake, and in this instance use the tools of redirection and coaching, which we discuss in Chapter 2.

The antecedent stage, once you can spot how it links to behavior, is one of the easier places to intervene and solve a problem *before* it happens.

Develop Awareness of Influences That Lead to Bad (and Good) Behavior

When you think about those factors that lead up to your child's behavior, keep in mind that there are an infinite number of conditions or influences that can contribute to them. These include temperament, expectations of behavior for your child's age, physical state, emotional state, as well as how he perceives himself.

It's important to remember that both short-term antecedents (those that happen immediately before the behavior) as well as long-term antecedents (those that happened at some point in the not-so-recent past) can lead to a behavior. Like adults, children can nurse a grudge or dredge up long-forgotten conflicts from the past, which can influence problem behavior today. Some of our own reasons for taking action may go back years in time; others may have been caused by an annoyance from a few moments before that put us in a bad mood. It's impossible to know everything that causes a behavior.

However, when looking at child behavior from the eyes of a parent, there are ways to target those contributing factors that have the *most* influence on an undesirable behavior. As a parent, you likely do this unconsciously, by knowing your child and using your instincts.

In order to truly utilize *Stress-Free Discipline*, we ask you to become more aware of these influences and how they affect your parenting approach. These influences can be both positive and negative, in terms of spurring behavior. We've broken them down into three broad categories, with examples, to help you connect them to your specific family challenges: situational influences, internal influences, and parental influences. All are ingredients in the soup that is behavior.

Situational Influences

Situational influences are circumstances that are actually happening at the time of the behavior. From causing an impulsive action to inhibiting a child from doing something, situational influences are "in the moment."

- *Temptation.* The availability of something your child wants but that you've restricted, such as a plate of cookies within reach on a counter, as opposed to the plate being up high where she can't access it.
- *People.* Individuals nearby can affect behavior, such as an authority figure who inhibits bad behavior, or friends who laugh and inadvertently reinforce silly or disruptive behavior.
- *Activities.* Lots of activities, or new activities, can mean competition for the child's attention, providing more potential reasons to ignore a parent's directive.

Internal Influences

Internal influences are those that stem from your child's thoughts and innate disposition. They may include forces of which you are unaware. Many of them are far less controllable than other influences (for example, you can't change temperament), but these factors should still be considered as you make your parenting decisions.

- *Temperament.* The child's innate characteristics that are forming his or her personality, such as how a competitive child argues a point further than one who is sensitive, and a risk-taker is more likely to push behavioral limits to the max.

- *Development.* Cognitive, physical, and emotional maturity can affect behavior, as when the child with greater self-esteem may be able to better understand her own motives or consequences and behave accordingly.
- *Knowledge.* What the child understands about the situation, such as the child who is used to getting in trouble and no longer responds to negative consequences, or the child in an unfamiliar setting who can't reason out the rules without explicit directions.

Parental Influences

Finally, we arrive at the type of influences on your child's behavior that stem from you. Moms and dads, we have *all* been there. Stressed out, had a bad day at work, got caught in traffic, you name it—there are many things that can compete with your attention and influence your child's behavior, as well as your reaction to that behavior. When your resources are reduced, you may not have the ability to pay attention to the factors that lead up to your child behaving badly.

- *Temperament.* You have your own temperament, or core personality (think Type A or Type B), that hardwires your responses to things like stress or problematic situations, which in turn affect your child's behavior.
- *Activities.* As with your children, the types and number of activities you take on in any given day can induce a wide variety of behaviors.
- *Support Level.* There are times when the level of support from a co-parent, spouse, or extended family changes, and this may affect the way you parent.

Chart Your Assets and Liabilities

Put a checkmark next to the asset or liability that describes you, and ask your spouse or co-parent to do the same. Then, add other assets or liabilities you see each of you possess at the end of the chart.

Assets and Liabilities	You	Co-Parent
Calm demeanor		
Tolerance		
Irritability/short fuse		
Rigid expectations		
Parenting for the first time		
Prior experience in parenting		
_____		
_____		
_____		
_____		
_____		

Finally, ask, "How does your partner respond to your weaknesses?," and answer by circling one of the following:

**IRRITATED   DISMISSIVE   NEUTRAL   SUPPORTIVE
TOTALLY IN SYNCH**

Use this chart to start a conversation with your spouse or co-parent and get on the same page in terms of your reactions to your child's attitude behaviors. As co-parents, you want to play to each other's strengths and minimize each other's weaknesses. Consistency and persistence are what will yield behavior improvements in your child.

Understand Your Child's Motives

"But," you ask, *"how can you be so sure my kids aren't intentionally trying to drive me crazy?"*

Not knowing your particular child or children, we can't be 100 percent positive, but knowing our own and many thousands of others makes us pretty sure they're just trying to find their way. Driving you crazy might be an entertaining fringe benefit, but it's not usually their main goal.

But what exactly *is* their main goal? They want what they want when they want it.

What follows are some generalizations about different age ranges, but they're commonalities that are true for most children.

Ages 3 and 4

In this age range, most children are self-centered. They feel like the world revolves around them. No one else matters except to help them get what they want, like a toy, a piece of food, or a destination. They want to get it, or get there. And that's developmentally appropriate—it's natural.

This is the core of why little kids don't share. They don't know they should, and they don't see any benefit to it. They haven't learned about perspective or empathy—that other people have feelings that should be considered. Part of the education (discipline) process for kids is to be guided by parents in developing these skills.

When you think of motives in children of this age, remember to keep perspective and focus on your child's actions. As an example, at the playground, your 3-year-old daughter grabs the swing away from another child. When it's pulled away, the other child loses his balance and falls down. She isn't intentionally trying to hurt the other child; she just sees something she wants and acts accordingly.

Focus on your child's action of grabbing the swing away, not necessarily on the fact that she hurt the other child. Explain how her actions affect others: "Use your words when you want something. If you'd talked with that boy instead of grabbing, you could have asked for the next turn and he wouldn't have gotten hurt. Let's go say 'sorry.'" Keeping your child's motivations in the forefront of your mind will help you with appropriate responses.

Ages 5 Through 7

In the 5-through-7 age range, goals shift a little. Children in this age range are starting elementary school and beginning to understand there are others around them. They're trying to figure out how they can leverage relationships to get preferred treatment—testing boundaries of how they're able to assert themselves, seeing how much advantage they can get in a certain situation.

Again, this is developmentally normal behavior, and frankly this is a trait to be prized. Balancing leverage is an important skill for successful adults. It's okay for children to be selfish at this age, but they should be learning how to consider those around them.

Also at this age, children are learning the value of intangible goals, such as achievement. They're looking to overcome a challenge and, in the case of the more competitive children, they're looking to achieve something faster, higher, or better than another child. The competitive side of things can get quite intense at this age. One thing they often compete for, which is crucial for you to understand if you have more than one child, is your attention.

A common refrain you'll hear is a claim of fairness. In some ways, this idea stems off as a variant of competition. Of course, the child's sense of fairness is usually skewed in his or her own favor. While something is "equitable" from the parent's perspective, it's almost never fair from the child's perspective.

Ages 8 Through 11

In the following few years, from ages 8 through 11, children begin to hone their persuasion skills, and their motivations may skew toward convincing you that they are right or that they should have what they want. (This, by the way, continues through adolescence and sometimes well into adulthood.) Again, this is perfectly natural, and a further extension away from egocentrism to perspective, but they are still refining the technique.

The child who learns to argue well to get what he wants is, in a way, learning to express the same sentiment as the one yanking the swing away from the other kid at the playground. Asserting their sense of self, children see themselves as having influence in the world, having power for the first time. They want to be important, and a way to do that is to manipulate or persuade others to their point of view.

Behavior = Communication

Rather than finding a *specific* motive to explain your child's behavior, you should consider the idea that from the toddler to the preteen years, behavior is often a means of *communication*. For example, for a child who gets frustrated and acts out may have no other motive than simply expressing frustration. She might not have any words she can use to express this feeling within herself adequately, so, instead, the behavior erupts to help release the emotion. This is no different from the off-color words that might escape our lips when we, say, crack the screen on our phone, find the dog got into the trash, or get cut off in traffic.

Expressing negative emotions through behavior is common. A child stamps her feet or slams the door; she's saying she's mad. Another child bursts into tears, rubs his eyes, and puts his head down; he's trying to say that he's tired, but he may not even know or admit it.

There's something cathartic about exploding that feels better than saying, "You know, Mom, the cookies are right there on the counter, and there seem to be plenty. I'm *frustrated* that you say I can't eat any of them right now." The refrain we've all heard and have likely said—"Use your words"—isn't always possible, and certainly doesn't feel as good. That's not to say we disagree with it, but simply to remind you that your children are also human beings, and human beings do explode from time to time.

Children can communicate exuberance or excitement through behavior as well, expressing even positive emotions through bad behavior. A super-giddy girl may spin throughout the house, her arms extended straight out, forgetting her parents' admonishments to watch out for that expensive vase on the counter until she hears it crash to the floor. In this case, unintended bad behavior was brought on by a positive motivation (happiness) she was trying to communicate through action.

When thinking about your child's motives, remember not to overcomplicate things. If your young child hits another child in response to being bumped, there may not be any real motive behind that action. The behavior may have looked "mean," but the intent was nothing more than impulsive retaliation. If it happens at school, however, he'll be in trouble whether the intent was there or not. Because older kids who hit often do it to be mean, we might assume the young child has the same intent. Try not to assume motivations. What we're trying to do is provide discipline (education) that helps our children change the way they deal with deep emotions away from behavior and into more appropriate methods of expression, like talking with a person about a problem.

> *Discipline (education) helps our children change the way they deal with deep emotions.*

With older children, motivation increases in stages, so while a 5-year-old may not have sophisticated motives behind hitting another, an 8-year-old may have more so. And a 10-year-old certainly has more.

This relates back to the idea of behavior as a choice. As adults, we're expected to be accountable for the choices we make. That's not to say that children shouldn't also be accountable. But children are often making far less informed choices than adults because they can't consider all of the factors or options available to them. They aren't capable of complex judgment in behavioral situations, so their motives can't be considered in the same vein as ours.

It's an important part of parenting and the establishment of discipline (education) to teach children to consider these various factors and consequences of behavior. Often, it's hard to remember how impulsive children are and that their motive for doing something may simply be "because it was there."

Just as essential, we parents *must* respect that our children are becoming people in their own right. They aren't our malleable little babies any longer, and we need to respect each child as an individual. That means that we try our hardest to understand their influences, motivations, and temperament so that we can decode their behavior and address it effectively. We protect our children as much as we can, but we allow them to make mistakes so they can learn from them. We encourage them to be considerate of us as actual people, too (instead of simply food providers or trash receptacles; right, moms?). When they can start doing that, they can have empathy for their siblings, friends, teachers, and classmates. Eventually, as they mature into the strong, healthy adults we're working so hard to produce, that empathy will extend to coworkers, neighbors, spouses, and their own children.

Helping your children begin to understand that their behavior has ramifications that need to be thought through is a long-term developmental process. But you're already on that road by using this book to help shape your child's behavior for the long term.

• • •

We've now taken you through the basic psychological understanding of your child's behavior, both good and bad. You've learned your ABCs, and know there are an infinite number of contributing factors that can influence your child toward choosing one behavior over another. We've discussed consequences and how they can shape behavior (both positively and negatively), and learned that antecedents are equally able to shape behavior but are unfortunately overlooked by many parents.

We've also explored situational, internal, and parental influences that are important to keep in mind as you think about your child's behavior. And, we've looked at motives.

Beyond all of this, every parent needs to remember that not all behavior is rational or understandable. This book is all about understanding your child, the circumstances that lead that child's behavior, as well as your own reactions to behavior. In short, we'll explain everything you need to know about behavior and how best to prepare for it and respond to it. But occasionally, all the information you have about what's going on in your child's life may not be enough for you to figure out why he did what he did. Sometimes there's just no real reason. It's okay if you can't figure it all out, and you shouldn't let that frustrate you to the point where you abandon your tactics. Chalking it up to "Kids these days!" and moving on is almost always the best bet.

2

Apply Universal Strategies

*H*ave you ever watched those reality shows on TV where the experienced nanny tells you how to parent your child the "right" way? There's always a super-simple concept with a cutesy name that single-handedly transforms a "problem" child into an angel within a convenient half-hour setting.

Have you then tried that super-simple concept at home, only to find it doesn't exactly work the same way on your children? There's either a mitigating factor that interferes with the tactic or your child reacts differently than the angel on TV. For many parents, this scenario of seeing or reading about a new strategy for discipline and trying it at home, only to have it fail, is a recurring cycle of frustration. What any of those TV shows, or magazine articles, or even other parenting books tries to sell you is their cutesy version of one of the strategies we're going to teach you in this chapter.

The difference with our book is that we're not going to sell you one of those strategies. We're going to *give* them to you, explain *why* they work, and then *teach* you how to implement them in your own home with your own children. If you understand the underlying principles, you can choose what will work for your specific situation.

These underlying principles are what we call *Universal Strategies*. They are the basic common denominators in parenting tactics that, to some extent, will work with most children. They will not all work for *all* kids in the same way; some will resonate better

> *Universal Strategies are the basic common denominator in parenting tactics.*

with your child than others, and that's typical. There are challenges with each. You'll need to take what we give you and apply it to your daughter or son, building on those tactics that resonate better and leaving the others in your back pocket.

Some of these strategies you may have already tried and abandoned, thinking they don't work for your child. While that may be the case, please keep an open mind and read through them all, because you might want to revisit them later. Understanding why each strategy works may help you implement it more effectively. Sometimes, a strategy you tried already may work later in a different situation. Having a good understanding of all of these strategies gives you options to deal with anything that comes up. There are no perfect methods and there are no guarantees as to which of our suggestions will spur *your* child to better behavior.

In this chapter, we outline some of the most commonly used Universal Strategies that will work with most children. Then, in the following chapters, we break them down even further and discuss the ways you can tailor them based on a specific problem at hand.

Cultivate a Positive Relationship with a Time-In

Time-In is the opposite of *Time-Out*, and what it basically means is that you cultivate a positive relationship with your child by spending time together. Some of you may look at this strategy and think, "*Duh!* We all know we should have a positive relationship with our children." But how does it affect your child's behavior? Having this kind of a foundation can be extremely powerful, both for averting a difficult situation and in dealing with one.

> *Your child must experience Time-In in order for Time-Out to work.*

A positive relationship gives you a favorable advantage and makes many of the other strategies we'll discuss in this book more effective and more potent. Your child will react more positively to your directions and reinforcements, will feel comfortable opening up his or her feelings to you, and will feel safe and secure in the parent–child relationship. Your child must experience Time-In in order for any Time-Out to work correctly as a negative consequence. Time-In needs to be meaningful in order to be used as leverage.

Make good use of your time, even if you don't have a lot of it. Use every moment together toward building a positive relationship with your child. You'll be surprised at how even the most routine activities can create opportunities for casual, stress-free communication with your child.

The BeThere campaign provides suggestions for just this sort of thing, taking what might have been a mundane moment in your day and turning it into a powerfully positive interaction with your child. You can find a number of videos to show you how it's done at www.bethere.org.

The more time you spend with your child, the more opportunities there are for her to talk about her life and experiences, which can provide insight into what she's thinking. As with adults, children often don't express their thoughts "on command." Instead, their inner thoughts leak out at various times, and we need to be available for those intimate moments.

When a child does share his emotions, parents need to validate those feelings and make an effort to understand the situation from the child's point of view. While you—as a rational adult—may grasp the reasons behind a rule or the purpose of a limitation, your child may likely only feel that it's unfair. It is very important that you show empathy for your child's emotional world. That doesn't mean you give in, just that you tell your child that you understand that he is upset, and communicate that he has a right to have that feeling if he expresses it in the proper way (in words, not as a tantrum).

But even in a family with the most positive relationships, a disciplinary issue may make those positive times feel futile. The negative can easily outweigh the positive in dark times, and that can become a vicious cycle unless you have this foundation of a positive relationship to fall back on. When your child trusts you, eventually she will come to you for help and let you into her world. If you set the stage for this now, the teen years will be much easier.

One key provision for a positive relationship: Allow for a clean slate each morning to avoid the buildup of frustration that may color your relationship. No matter how many behavior problems happened yesterday, today wipes the record clean. Your child must know that you love him no matter what and that he still has a reason to try to succeed today.

Role-Model Good Behavior

Children learn everything by watching: Their little eagle eyes miss nothing. Their world revolves around us, and so very often we are teaching them behaviors without even knowing it. That's where this strategy comes in. Showing is more powerful than telling. Sometimes, the best way to get your children to do something is to do it yourself when you know they are watching. Role-modeling good behavior helps your children avoid bad behavior because you are communicating through action what you want them to do.

> *We are teaching them behaviors without even knowing it.*

If you stop at a crosswalk and wait for the signal before crossing, your children will learn to do the same. If you clean up messes without complaining, that's what they'll (eventually) do. If you put away your cell phone at dinnertime, they'll learn that's the way things work in your home. If you treat salespeople and waiters with respect, using *please* and *thank you*, your children will know that's how they're supposed to behave.

Sometimes, good behavior occurs right away as an immediate mimic; other times, it takes a while for the behavior to seep into a child's consciousness. Teachable moments can be positive in and of themselves, or be a negative situation turned into a positive lesson. Take a circumstance that irritates you, and be obvious in the ways you calm yourself down: Take a loud, deep breath, validate your own emotion, and, out loud, talk yourself through letting go of the aggravation. When your children overhear you talking through your emotions, they will internalize those lessons and apply them to themselves when they face a similar situation. Keep in mind, though, that this strategy works both ways. Your kids will copy both your good and bad behavior. Unfortunately, it's the bad behaviors that can be most memorable, usually because they're a little more dramatic. If you curse and pound on the horn in traffic, your children will believe that's the way to handle frustration while driving. If you talk trash about the neighbors, your children will think that's how they should treat others. If you argue with the referee at the youth soccer game, your kids will think that's how to be a good coach.

Role-modeling also extends to mistakes. If you want your kids to learn from the mistakes they make, you need to do the same. When you make a mistake, and we *all* do, don't dwell on it. Be a role model to your child in coping with having made a mistake: Own it, apologize for it, and don't make it the next time.

Prioritize Your Absolutes

As parents, you will have *Absolutes*—behaviors you absolutely expect from family members. They reflect your values and thus are different for every family. There are no right or wrong items for you and your spouse to put on this list.

Here's what an Absolute means: You will absolutely not tolerate a behavior and will stop what you're doing to address that issue immediately, taking decisive action and brooking no explanations. These are the lines in the sand that, when crossed, provoke a reaction that conveys to your child that he has gone too far. Absolute means absolutely consistent: *Every time* this behavior happens, you are resolute and take action in response. Coordinate and predetermine your response with any other adult who helps to parent your child.

> *Keep your family's list of absolutes very short.*

Keep your family's list of Absolutes very short. These are things you're going to go to the mat for, and if you choose too many, you'll be on the mat too often. You won't be able to effectively parent with such rigid parameters. For example, in many families, hitting is never tolerated. If you and your spouse determine that will be one of your Absolutes, then every time you see your child hit someone, you *always* need to react with a consequence. Many families use a swift Time-Out in these cases.

Give Good Directions

Children need simple, clear, well-thought-out directions, and often more specifics than we adults realize. Miscommunication can be a frequent cause of your child getting into a disciplinary situation.

Learning to give good directions reduces miscommunications and frustration as well as avoids some problem situations. Being able to successfully follow your directions helps build your child's sense of his or her own competence, which is important for developing self-esteem.

Here are some tips on how to give effective directions:

- Ensure you have your child's attention. This means turning off the TV or getting in between your child and whatever electronic gadget is in front of him.

- Break your directions down step by step: First do this; next do that; then this, and so on.
- Offer a positive outcome, using *if/then* and *when/then* statements, which tie an outcome to a behavior. For example: "*When* you finish picking up your toys, *then* we will be able to go meet friends at the park."
- Have your child repeat the instructions back to you or paraphrase them to ensure they are understood.
- Finish with praise, even if you had to help them complete the task.

Enforce Limits and Rules

Children must be aware of boundaries and expectations. The clash between what your child wants and where you have set limits is a flashpoint for behavioral situations. This struggle is a natural manifestation of growth and development, and family conflicts are very normal. Enforcing the limits you've determined are appropriate for your child is a key strategy, one you've likely already tried to implement. If you had mixed results in terms of getting your child to stay within the limits you've set, then this is a strategy you'll want to use.

First, make sure you've explained your rules. Use the tips from the Universal Strategy of giving good directions to ensure your child understands them. Second, role-model this behavior, especially as your child is younger and first learning it. Third, make sure to embed a positive reinforcement, an incentive, for a job well done that is appropriate for this rule. (Example: After dinner, the rule is that your child clears the table. Once the table is cleared, dessert can be served.) Be consistent so your children know this is a set rule they must always abide by. And, finally, praise them when they do a good job and follow the rules.

Enforcing limits is an extension of those rules. Here is how to follow through on limits:

- Firmly, but politely, tell your children they've reached their limit.
- Remind them what they need to do at this point (i.e., turn off the TV, come in from playing outside, do their homework, etc.).
- Give them a chance to follow your directions. Don't give them too long—just enough as is appropriate to whatever activity is involved at that moment.
- If your children follow your directions, use positive reinforcement/praise.
- If they did not follow your directions, step in and enforce the limit yourself. (Some parents give a warning, which is okay.)
- Depending on the situation and your child's age, a consequence may be warranted. Most often, a natural, negative consequence is appropriate: "Since you weren't able to turn off the TV on your own when I told you to, I'm going to have to hold onto the remote control and do it for you next time."

Allowing your children to make their own mistakes—reach your limits, go over them, and suffer a consequence—is a necessary part of parenting. It's never fun, but this underscores the need for consistency. Your children will learn faster when you have clear rules and enforce consistent limits.

Please don't misunderstand. We're not saying that the first time you detail your expectations to your children they will comply. All of this takes time and plenty of repetition. When your children know what to expect and where those limits are, they will *eventually* act accordingly.

Redirect Your Child's Focus

Redirection is a strategy that you can use to defuse a situation before it explodes. Basically, when you see a problem about to start, you redirect your child to another activity and thereby avoid the problem altogether.

This strategy with younger children is a valuable lesson, because if your child can begin redirecting himself, he will find as he gets older, he will be more prepared to avoid many problems of adolescence, such as peer pressure, cliques in school, or even fights.

By watching a child or a group of children, you can get a sense as to when an activity needs to change. With younger children, it may often be that when they're playing with toys, and one toy becomes the focus of the entire group, you may have to redirect a child who's already had a turn with that toy to another toy, thus enabling his friend to have a turn. When kids are a little older, it may be that you sense the game of tag in the backyard is getting out of balance because the biggest, fastest kid has won too many rounds. At that point, suggesting a snack or bringing out another game for them to play will allow for a change of focus.

A key challenge is making that new toy or activity attractive enough to steal your child's attention away from the potentially problematic situation. The most strategic parents will hold something like a snack or a different toy back until a potential problem crops up, and then bring it out at the proper moment.

Act Like a Coach

In many cases, acting like a coach can be a winning strategy as a parent because it both educates and sets positive behaviors in motion, which create helpful antecedents. Coaches cheer their athletes, but at the same time point out what skills need to be worked on.

The coaching strategy is made up of a discussion with your child just before getting into a situation that's known to be troublesome. You need to be *very specific* in terms of naming the behavioral tendencies your child has had in similar situations in the past that concern you.

For example, if your child tends to get wound up and act crazy in a group situation, you need to be proactive and say exactly that: "We are going to John's birthday party, and sometimes when you are in a big group of excited children you run around and knock other children over. If you are going to do that, we can't stay at the party. Do you understand?"

You are soliciting your child's agreement that he will work to manage the behavior that you have very specifically named. It's helpful to prompt him again just as he is entering the situation, and even *during* the situation once or twice if necessary. You take what would otherwise be an impulsive behavior and bring it to his conscious awareness before the behavior occurs, and then keep him thinking about it throughout the entire situation. The idea is that he'll then be more likely to self-manage that behavior.

Letting your child know that you have had the same emotion she is having is a powerful lesson.

A good technique for validating your child's feelings in a coaching setting is to personalize your empathy: "I understand how you feel; when I was a kid, the same thing happened to me, and I didn't like it very much." Letting your child know that you have had the same emotion she is having is a powerful lesson. This is central to the idea of shaping your child's behavior in a positive direction. In using validating statements, you're identifying with her emotions, and then coaching her on how to keep her behavior under control despite having these emotions.

Keep in mind that the more difficult the behavior, the more planning and coaching needs to occur. And just like coaching a sports team, your children aren't necessarily going to get every concept the first time. You have to keep coaching them through those difficult situations again and again, continuing to provide positive reinforcement, and also have some post-game meetings. The great coaches move forward from a loss, taking what they can learn and applying it in the next game.

Hold Practice Sessions

This strategy is for situations that give you or your child trouble. Practice sessions can be held for anything: a trip to the grocery store, a meal in a restaurant, or even calming down after a tantrum. This strategy goes hand in hand with the Universal Strategy of coaching.

Start by explaining you noticed she had trouble the last time she tried this activity. So you want to show her how it's done and give her some practice time. Give her your full attention, with no other children around, and practice at a time when you have no scheduled activities or deadlines. Go through the entire situation and use key points to explain important considerations, but if things get heated or your child slips into the problem behavior, you are ready to bail out.

The beauty of practice sessions is that they build familiarity with the situation for both you and your child. If all goes well, they give your child a positive, successful experience that you can then remind her of before the next "real" situation. These sessions give you a calm setting in which to show your child what to expect during this situation. They also give you an opportunity to explain how you want to see your child behave in spite of any upsetting feelings she may experience during this situation. Another benefit to practice sessions is that they allow you to practice keeping your priorities in perspective when facing a potential behavior problem. You will learn just as much from these practice sessions as your child in terms of managing your own responses.

Using this strategy, the practice needs to be the *only* focus. In other words, when dinner is late and you have to pick up a few things at the grocery store, this is *not* the time to practice going to the store with your child. (You can read a step-by-step account of a grocery store practice session in Chapter 3.) Practice sessions can be a big time commitment, but this is also one of the most helpful strategies for parents and children.

Practice sessions are one of the most helpful strategies for parents and children.

Ignore the Problem Behavior

Ignoring problem behavior involves a little reverse psychology. If an antecedent and consequence make it more or less likely that a behavior will be repeated, then the absence of either should have the opposite effect.

In other words, sometimes getting your attention in any way, bad or good, can be reinforcing to your child, thereby making it more likely that the behavior will occur again in the future. So, when your child doesn't get any attention for a behavior, often he will stop doing it. At the very least, ignoring a behavior

is a neutral factor; it avoids escalation and doesn't reinforce anything. It also allows you to remain
consistent in your responses.

Has your child ever had a tantrum in an empty room?

Has your child ever had a
tantrum in an empty room? No;
the point of a tantrum is to get
your attention and draw you into an emotional drama. This is
why it's so crucial to understand the ABCs of behavior. Ignoring
is best used when your attention, or reaction, is reinforcing to the
behavior, or when your child's behavior doesn't engage you.

For example, let's say you observe your child getting upset
with a friend at a playdate and come whining to you. You do
have the option of stepping in. However, if you choose to ignore
the whining, your child is forced to turn his attention back to his
friend and the kids may now work out their problem and keep
playing. In this case, you have refused to reinforce the behavior
of whining, and the consequence of the kids working it out on
their own will naturally reinforce problem-solving the next time
they have a disagreement. Note that using the ignoring strategy
on behaviors you do not want to reinforce does not mean that
you ignore the children. In this situation, parents need to keep
their eyes (or ears) open to ensure the disagreement they are
having doesn't escalate. If the kids start to yell at each other or
hit each other, you will need to intervene.

Here's a different example: If your child is using foul language, your reaction may simply reinforce the behavior and
make it more likely that your child repeats the behavior. Getting
upset and making a big to-do about a bad word feeds the situation, because the child gets a great deal of attention for his behavior. Ignoring is the neutral factor because it doesn't reinforce
anything. Your child gets no attention and is likely to stop saying

that bad word. Of course, the age of the child plays a huge factor in cursing, and this must be taken into account as well.

It is hard work to *not* take action sometimes, but in certain instances, pretending to not notice a behavior and doing nothing can be the best strategy.

Disengage from Behavior Out of Your Control

Disengaging is the art of responding appropriately to behavior that's out of your control without escalating a problem. It's not ignoring, but instead a neutral, superficial response that does not feed into the heightened emotions and charged behaviors of a difficult situation. Typically, at these times, your child is trying to draw you into the fray, and disengaging is a way to respond without adding fuel to the fire. It works because you're not inadvertently reinforcing negative behavior.

> *Disengaging is a way to respond without adding fuel to the fire.*

The typical sequence is that your child argues and you argue back. But what is the point of that? If you engage in an argument with your child, you often add to the emotion of the situation, which won't go well, *and* you reinforce her arguing with your attention. Basically, we're buying ourselves *more* arguments from our kids, rather than fewer.

Use automatic responses to disengage. The response, *"I understand that,"* is a terrific phrase you can use when, for example, your child is upset about a rule or a direction. That statement places the burden back on the child to decide how to act to fix whatever is the problem and does not rope you into taking responsibility for anything other than understanding your child's feelings.

If your child tries to draw you into an argument about whatever she is unhappy about, instead of repeatedly answering her with *no*, you can politely but matter-of-factly respond with, "I've already told you. . . ." Each time your child asks, you provide the same short, calm response. The idea from a behavioral standpoint is that you reduce the frequency of the child's behavior by simply not engaging, which provides no reinforcement to arguing.

CHILD: *I don't want to go upstairs and brush my teeth. I want to finish watching this TV show!*
YOU: *I understand that.*
CHILD: *It's my favorite show.*
YOU: *I understand that. It's your favorite show. But it's bedtime.*
CHILD: *So why can't I watch it till the end?*
YOU: *I already told you, it's bedtime.*
CHILD: *But it's a really good show!*
YOU: *I understand that. But what did I already tell you?*

You have to stick with this strategy, as well as your composed demeanor. You can't get angry, and you can't use an automatic response five times and then give in on the sixth because that reinforces the behavior more strongly than if you'd just given in the first time. Plus, that only teaches your child that if she keeps at you, she can get you to change your behavior.

Yell Sparingly

If used very sparingly, yelling can let your children know immediately that whatever they are doing is serious and they need to *STOP RIGHT NOW.*

The word *sparingly* is a key distinction. While so many of us go straight to yelling as a first reaction, what that does is de-values the yell as an attention grabber, so that eventually your child doesn't even pay attention to it. If everything sounds the same, your child has no way to differentiate what is a really important limit from something that is not a big deal in the grand scheme of things. When something really serious does happen, there's no higher level you can go to in order to convey that seriousness and urgency.

> *You want to be able to pull out your Code Red tactic when you need it.*

It's crucial that you have something in your parenting tool box that signals Code Red and that your child will know not to ignore you. Yelling can be that strategy. With small children, it might be yelling when they're about to run into the road. With older children, it could be, "*Don't touch* that hot stove!" You want to be able to pull out your Code Red tactic when you need it and be 100 percent certain it will get his attention.

Praise Positive Behavior

Praise is a simple strategy. It calls for carefully chosen words that call out specific behaviors in order to meaningfully reinforce what you see your child doing right. Used correctly, praise is a consequence, and a powerful one at that. It can also become a positive antecedent, something that contributes to future stellar behavior.

Look for ways to catch your children being good, and then praise them for the behavior you see. It may be that this is new behavior they're exhibiting, in which you can express happiness and perhaps congratulations on a skill they've developed. "I see some very nice sharing going on with your brother today. I like to see that!"

But it's possible that your child is now showing you good behavior after learning his or her lesson about bad behavior in the past, and that warrants well-deserved kudos, as well. Here's how to tweak the way you use praise to acknowledge progress from your child: "I saw how nice you were sharing toys with your brother. I know it's difficult for you to let him use some of your special toys, and I can see how hard you're working at it. Great job, honey!"

Praise as an antecedent works like this: At first it's a consequence of doing something good; it is then carried over and remembered by your child before the next similar situation, which makes it more likely he or she will behave well again.

The most powerful praise is *immediate, specific, and sincere:* immediate, in that it takes place in a reasonable amount of time directly after the display of good behavior; specific, because your child wants to know exactly what she did well—which means praising those things that the child can control (effort, persistence, resilience, etc.) instead of those things she can't (intelligence, beauty, etc.); and sincere, because a kid can spot a fake from a mile away.

> *The most powerful praise is immediate, specific, and sincere.*

Third-party praise can be extraordinarily potent as well. Brag about how your children did something great to someone who wasn't there. This can be a spouse, grandparent, or friend.

You can do this in front of your children, or even when you know they'll overhear you, such as when you're on the phone:

You: *Hi, Mom, guess what your granddaughter did today? She was outside playing with her friends and saw me pull in with the groceries. She stopped playing and came right over to help carry the bags inside. What a thoughtful girl, and such a hard worker!*

Surprise praise, or intermittent praise, can be an extremely powerful reinforcement, as well. Telling your child, out of the blue, that you like something he did, at a time in which there's no expressed need for praise, will generate positive results for a long while. Psychologists call this *intermittent reinforcement*, referring to the unpredictable intervals at which the reinforcement is given. That it is unexpected is what triggers a very strong drive in the child's brain to achieve that kind of reinforcement, or praise, again.

It's important to learn what kind of praise is most reinforcing to your child. Some kids like quiet praise, even just a pat on the shoulder. Others like the bigger celebration—whooping and high-fiving. Despite your own personal preferences, you need to fit the praise to your child's tastes, or you run the risk of your praise backfiring to make it less likely he or she will repeat the behavior in the future. A common example of this is making such a huge to-do about something that you embarrass your quiet, shy child, who makes a mental note to never succeed so well again in order to avoid this uncomfortable feeling.

Appropriate kinds of praise should be used liberally, but don't praise to the point that it loses its meaning and potency. Avoid superlatives like *best* or *perfect* because they ring hollow to children. Too much praise can be counterproductive, as the child can't separate what is meaningful praise from those positive words that Mom or Dad always use about everything.

Offer Positive Reinforcement or Rewards

Positive reinforcement can be among the most effective behavioral tools in your parental tool box. Tangible rewards that parents use, such as candy, toys, or stickers, are a form of positive reinforcement, but giving accolades has more long-term benefits. Both are that carrot, dangling out there in front of a child, who can sense the benefit to herself and will strive to reach it. When you read through this strategy, remember the word *reward* can mean verbal recognition or something tangible.

> *Reward can mean verbal recognition or something tangible.*

There are many children for whom a regular schedule of goals and rewards are what keeps them on track because they learn to associate a positive behavior with a positive outcome. Some children really thrive with a very structured routine of what to do when and what rewards they'll get for certain behaviors. The clinical phrase for this when discussing behaviorism is "rewards at regular intervals."

A reward chart is the most common example. To create a chart, you need to list the expected behaviors and actions you want your child to do, and then mark off every time he does them. The reward is a goal for achieving a number of marks within a certain time frame. So, let's say you make out a list of chores and good behaviors for your child, and every time he accomplishes one, you put a gold star on the chart. The child's aim might be to get 10 gold stars a week to earn the reward of going the movie theater that weekend. The idea of a rewards chart can be amended in a plethora of ways to work for your family's particular situation. Just be aware that some kids will try to game this system, and if that happens in your home, you may want to consider using recognition and rewards in different ways.

Other children will respond most strongly to "rewards at unexpected intervals." For them, the timing of the positive outcome is what creates the potency. Studies have shown that surprise benefits have the most power and that when a reward comes out of nowhere, it reinforces whatever behavior it's associated with and cements that in the child's mind.

This means that you really have to be careful in how you implement a reward. One way to do this is to wait to see the good behavior that you want to reinforce, and then drop the reward into the child's lap: "Fantastic job on your science project! I want to see you do more of that kind of work, so I've decided that microscope you wanted from the store the other day might be a really good idea. Let's go get it and see how it works!"

A less effective approach is saying something like, "If you do great on your science project, I'll buy you that microscope you wanted." Rewards that are contingent on actions are a slippery slope: Pretty soon the child will demand a prize before doing anything that's outside of his or her interest area. That's not to mention the definition of "doing great" may be different in your child's mind from what you had in mind.

Use Negative Consequences Through Punishment

As with any skill that has to be developed, there will be the normal setbacks and slipups as your child learns good behavior. We

don't immediately punish a child
who makes mistakes while learning to read; instead, we correct
the mistakes, we teach over and
over again, and we praise effort
and eventual success. Please know
that punishment is *one* method
of trying to control your child's
behavior, but as we've learned in
this chapter, it's by no means the
only method.

Punishment is one method of trying to control your child's behavior, but it's by no means the only method.

In the ABC concept of behavior, punishment falls into the category of implementing negative consequences, which make it less likely your child will repeat the behavior. You want to cause some displeasure, enough so that your child will remember that feeling when he or she is at the juncture of a similar situation and making a decision about how to act. You want your child to associate bad behavior with a negative outcome.

How do you know you're choosing the right negative consequence? Oh, you'll know you've stumbled into an effective negative consequence when you hit on something that causes a great deal of displeasure. The most effective negative consequence is different for each child.

Just as the praise strategy calls for carefully chosen actions that call out specific behaviors in order to meaningfully reinforce what you see your child doing right, negative consequences should be carefully chosen to respond to specific behaviors in order to reinforce against their happening again.

The most powerful negative consequence is *immediate, specific, and within the context* of the behavior you're trying to stop. And just as you can overdo praise until it loses its value, you can overdo punishments as well. If overused, the displeasure your child feels can turn to a feeling of futility, and then the punishment loses its potency. If your child always loses his favorite toy as a consequence for bad behavior, pretty soon that toy won't be the favorite anymore and taking it away won't have any effect on his behavior. You need to avoid overreliance on a handful of negative consequences and change them up from time to time to keep them useful.

Regardless of how often you use it, the type of negative consequence needs to logically relate in some way to the behavior you're punishing. If your son throws a toy at his sibling, he loses that toy. If your daughter rides her bike to a friend's house without wearing a helmet, she loses the privileges of going to her friend's house for the weekend and riding her bike.

A great way to be effective using negative consequences with your children is to follow up an hour, day, or week (depending on the circumstances) later with praise that is directly related to their behavior since they experienced the negative consequence: "Honey, I like to see how you put your helmet on every time you ride your bike now, without me even reminding you. I know it was hard to be grounded last weekend, but you've really learned that safety is important, and I'm proud of you." By pairing the negative consequence with subsequent praise, you're shaping their behavior twice, and pointing them toward the behavior you want to see more of in the future. The pairing also reinforces the idea of starting out each day with a clean slate.

By pairing the negative consequence with subsequent praise, you're shaping their behavior twice.

Punishments can go beyond causing displeasure, however. Spanking, for example, is a severely negative consequence that causes pain. While it interrupts a bad behavior at that moment, psychological research does *not* support its benefit as a parenting strategy. It really does not increase positive behavior and decrease negative behavior. Further, there are risks involved with spanking, which can lower your child's self-esteem, academic achievement, peer relationships, conflict resolution skills, and so on.

Call a Time-Out

A Time-Out is one of the most used, and in some cases, overused discipline strategies available to parents. Too often, it's the go-to response when something else might have worked better. It is a valid tool, but perhaps not for the reasons you may think.

A Time-Out is a negative consequence for a behavior: Your child loses the ability to be around family and friends for a period of time. It interrupts whatever he is doing and allows for a cool-down period. But in order for this to work as a negative reinforcement, to make it more likely the behavior will not be repeated, your child has to have the positive context of a Time-In. The leverage here is the relationship and positive attention the child is accustomed to receiving, and the loss thereof. The Time-Out strategy goes hand-in-hand with the Time-In strategy of cultivating a positive relationship. "It seems like you're having a hard time being careful in the pool. I've already warned you to be more careful, so now you need to go inside and have a Time-Out. When you're ready to follow the rules, you can come back outside and swim with us again. I'll set the timer for five minutes."

Remember, children are looking for attention. If your child gets attention for bad behavior, and you spend more time with her, she will continue to try to get that attention. If you spend more time with her when she is behaving well, she will continue along those lines.

A Time-Out can be in the child's room, in a corner, on the stairs, anywhere. That detail isn't what makes the strategy. You can find a breakdown of giving a Time-Out during a tantrum in Chapter 3.

In younger children, a Time-Out has a mystique about it. They link it with punishment and getting fussed at, and so some kids respond even if a Time-In is not all that great. But especially as kids get a little older, the Time-In component is what gives the Time-Out its potency. This is why starting early to develop that positive, happy family relationship is crucial to all discipline methods.

Insist on an Apology and Restitution

Whether accidental or intentional, if your child's behavior causes harm or inconvenience to another person—child or adult—then a follow-up apology and restitution should be implemented. He needs to say he's sorry, and needs to make it right, whether that's paying for a broken toy or cleaning up a mess. Restitution can take many forms and should be undertaken by your child as a natural consequence of his actions.

Moreover, it's important to consider restitution not so much as a consequence for behavior (though having to clean up multiple accidental spills may be noxious enough to the child to make her be a little more careful), but as something that is the *right* thing to do. You're guiding your child to develop greater empathy and consideration of others. "When you broke Dylan's toy, you didn't realize it was a favorite from his grandfather, and you need to make it right. That toy costs twenty dollars at the store,

> *He needs to say he's sorry and make it right.*

so you're going to need to do enough chores around the house to earn that money to replace Dylan's toy. We're going to walk next door, and I want you to tell Dylan that you're sorry and that you'll get him a new one."

The idea of apologizing and making something right often brings up the concept of *intent*. Have you had your children say they are sorry, perhaps to a sibling, but they roll their eyes and say it in such a way that it is obvious they don't mean it? It is so frustrating. You want your children to mean it because that shows they're actually developing that empathy and consideration we want them to acquire.

There's a saying that psychologists often tell parents: "Parent the behavior, not the intent." The intent will follow, eventually, as your child matures. You cannot force someone to feel something, but you can force him or her to say something. Sometimes restitution and apology really just take your child through the motions, but it's necessary nonetheless.

•••

There are strong emotions on all sides when dealing with a behavioral situation. By understanding the ABCs and the ways in which these Universal Strategies work, you can keep your focus on helping to shape your child's behavior positively toward appropriate ways to handle a situation.

Kids will say mean things sometimes; often they are simply communicating their vexation in the only way they know how. So when your child says, "I hate you," or "I won't invite you to my birthday party," what you should hear is, "You're making me mad," and "I want you to know how angry I am." Try not to take any of this personally and use the strategy of disengaging. (But please realize these words can be deeply wounding to siblings or friends, so you'll need to make this clear if your child uses them toward another child.)

All of these Universal Strategies are adaptable to your specific situation and can be mixed and matched with each other to give you an unlimited number of parenting tactics. Some of them will work better than others for a particular child. Some will work better than others for a particular issue, such as tantrums, homework, or bedtime. In Part II of *Stress-Free Discipline*, we take you through some specific examples of how to implement these strategies within the context of common disciplinary problem areas.

PART II

Dealing with Areas of Common Difficulty

3

Tantrums

When your child throws a temper tantrum, it can cut right to your core. What goes through your mind can run the gamut from bewilderment at the cause of the tantrum, to embarrassment if the tantrum takes place in public, to frustration if you cannot make it stop.

Let's begin by examining the causes of a tantrum. When a tantrum occurs, it typically stems from your child's sense of frustration or anger. There is something she wants but cannot have, or something he sees but cannot touch. Sometimes, your child is watching other children do something that he cannot do, either because he's not allowed to do it or he can't yet manage it physically.

Anger is a natural emotion we all experience. Anger can be adaptive, because it alerts us that something may not be right or

> *Anger is a natural emotion we all experience.*

that we might be in danger. We communicate our anger through actions, behaviors, and language. Some of our responses to anger are simply a matter of nature; human beings have physiologic responses that can include increased heart rate, faster breathing, blushing, and so on. In children, the anger response can often manifest as a tantrum.

In this chapter, we take a look at the source of temper tantrums, again offering that peek inside your child's brain. We talk about typical triggers of tantrums and how to manage them. Tips for how to handle a tantrum, and a step-by-step example of using the coaching and practice session strategies at the grocery store will follow. Toward the end, we take you through what to do if your child's tantrum becomes violent and give you some ideas for resetting your relationship if you feel like it's turned negative.

Understand the Source of Tantrums by Age

Tantrums can occur at any age; we've even seen some terrible adult tantrums. However, it's often that time frame aptly called the "Terrible Twos" that launch them in children. At the age of two, children do not have the words or the understanding of how to use the words they know to describe their feelings, so it's up to you to help them through it. The third year can be similar, as their words can't keep up with the pace of their exploration of the world around them. There are plenty of parents who find that the threes are even worse than the twos they thought were so terrible.

From the ages of four until about six, the tantrums are morphing into a bit less of a self-centered tirade, but your child is still learning how to use words and to regulate his emotions. Tantrums may become a little more strategic in nature. As mentioned in Chapter 1, kids at this age are trying to figure out how they can leverage relationships to their advantage and testing boundaries to see how they can assert themselves. They are also very much still learning how to express their feelings in appropriate ways.

Between the ages seven and nine, a tantrum may be more a first foray into rebellion, and certainly may contain a bit more anger than frustration. Children at this age have words, but still may not be able to translate their feelings into words. They are under a great deal more pressure as they get older, and for some children, just like for some people of any age, there is a need to occasionally blow their stack to release that pressure. Some of us are just hardwired to fly off the handle more easily than others, so consider your child's personality in determining why his tantrums persist.

> *Some of us are just hardwired to fly off the handle more easily than others.*

At 10 and 11, kids are approaching the tween years and often want to separate themselves from their parents as much as possible. You may find attitude to be constant, and they can be dismissive of your parental protection or knowledge. Social and academic pressures are higher at this age. They look outward to friends and social groups to gather information about the world around them. For some, puberty has already started or is coming soon, and with that comes hormones that can play havoc with emotions. Children at this age may understand what they are feeling but can be confused as to why they are feeling that way.

Manage Contributing Factors

Many tantrums are simple and impulsive. Your child has a want, a limit is set, and the child expresses frustration and anger by way of a tantrum. In many instances, it really is no more compli-cated than that. So managing the "wants" is an antecedent man-agement strategy.

The first question you need to ask yourself when you see a tantrum begin is: "Is my child hungry or tired?" Those triggers alone will account for many tantrums in children of all ages. Keeping an emergency snack on hand can go a long way toward preventing, or at least reducing, a tantrum. (Sara has a hidden granola bar in every purse, every car, and in nearly every bag for this express purpose.)

There's no hiding a nap in a purse, though. If your child falls asleep in the aftermath of a tantrum, then you'll know what induced it. The only cure for being overtired is sleep. Any time your child is off his or her sleep schedule because of a busy day, try to make the time spent in your car as conducive to a nap as possible. Also, try to make sure the following day adheres to your child's usual sleep schedule.

What are you doing with these snacks and naps? You're trying to manage the factors that contribute to a tantrum—those things that make it more likely for a behavior to occur. By mini-mizing them, you can remove, or at least reduce, the likelihood of a full-blown tantrum. While hun-ger and being tired are two com-mon triggers, there are plenty of others.

> *By minimizing the antecedents, you can remove, or reduce, the likelihood of a tantrum.*

The second question you need to ask yourself is, "Am I tak-ing my child into a situation that may be likely to provoke a tantrum?" If so, see if there's a way you can help your child avoid that situation: Skip the third birthday party of the weekend, or go to the grocery store later when your child isn't in tow. Advance thought will help you to either avoid a potential tantrum or be prepared for its occurrence. If you still must go into a provocative situation, using the Universal Strategies of redirection and coaching discussed in Chapter 2 will be most helpful.

The beginnings of an illness can also be the cause of a behavioral problem that seems to come out of nowhere. A fever or sore throat the following day can clue you into the reasons behind the previous day's bad behavior.

Sometimes, you can see your child start to get upset. If you can catch your child before the tantrum takes hold and name the feelings she may be having, that simple act of validating her emotional state can sometimes be enough to head off the tantrum. The anger a child shows can often be connected to the perception that no one understands what they are feeling. If you express understanding of her point of view, it may help take the wind out of the sails of a stormy tantrum.

That simple act of validating her emotional state can sometimes be enough.

There are situational influences that can cause a tantrum as well. Perhaps your child is not getting enough exercise or is reacting to something bad happening at school. Traveling or sitting in a waiting room for long periods of time can also trigger fussiness and tantrums. Having a bag of tricks, such as crayons or a little game, in your purse or car can be helpful, but what you really need is to be watchful and mindful of the effect of these influences on your child. Allowing your child to stretch his legs as often as you can will help. Using some of their weekly limit of screen time on a mobile device during the wait may also be worth it. Getting a hint of a specific trigger will go a long way toward helping you prevent your child's tantrums.

Consider whether you can reduce the demands on your child. Try to keep the child's environment calm and not overly competitive. If your child appears tense, a little extra attention may prevent an eventual angry outburst.

Prepare your child *in advance* for changes in activity by explaining why a play schedule must be interrupted or why a request is being denied. Use the coaching strategy after your explanation, being very explicit in describing the tantrum behavior you do not want to see: "Sometimes, when we're leaving the playground where you've been having fun, you scream and yell and cry that you don't want to leave. Do you think today you can come with me without doing that?"

If your child agrees, then you go to the playground and give her ample warnings as you approach the end of your time there. Remind her of your agreement, and tell her that the consequences of breaking it will mean no playground time the next day. If, however, your child says no when you ask if she can avoid the tantrum when leaving, then you just simply stay home.

As your child gets older, you can build in positive reinforcement for not having a tantrum. For example, you can offer praise after a high-risk episode in which your child did not have a tantrum. Specific praise, such as "I know you were getting really frustrated and angry back there, but you did such a good job of using your words! I'm so proud of you!" shows your child that you don't take his effort at regulating his emotions for granted.

Finally, sometimes you simply may not recognize that there are patterns to your child's tantrums. In other words, there may be contributing factors that are controllable or consequences that are reinforcing the tantrums, but you don't initially see them.

Log Tantrums

If your child has repeated tantrums, you should keep a log of the ABCs. Include:

The time of day relative to naps and meals: _____

What was happening prior to the tantrum: _____

_____

_____

What situation the child was about to go into or what situation

she was being asked to leave: _____

_____

_____

Which people were around: _____

What happened during the tantrum: _____

_____

_____

What happened after the tantrum: _____

_____

_____

Reflections on whether you could have done something

differently: _____

_____

_____

With a log of this nature, you can look for common denominators in terms of ABCs. Once some of those repeating triggers are identified, you can make adjustments that may prove helpful in preventing and effectively managing future tantrums.

Deal with Tantrums

But what if you don't catch wind of the oncoming storm? Sometimes a tantrum can really come out of nowhere. Children don't yet know the words to describe their emotions when these frustrating or maddening situations arise, so they act them out instead. That acting out can range from a thunderstorm to a full-on hurricane, depending on the situation and your child's personality.

Once a tantrum starts, it is maintained by attention. Despite the severity of the tantrum, your goal in handling it is to let your child know that this kind of behavior will get him or her absolutely nowhere. Children need to talk about their feelings of anger rather than lashing out verbally or physically. Your job is to teach them how to do that, with the understanding that the process of their learning this skill is a gradual one that occurs over time, and through constant repetition.

Your goal is to let your child know this behavior will get her nowhere.

Using the Universal Strategy of role-modeling will lay a foundation for dealing with your child's tantrums. While a tantrum may be a physiologic response to anger, kids learn how to manage this emotion by watching how adults (starting with Mom and Dad) deal with it. So before you start in with any attempts to teach your child how to express his or her feelings with words instead of anger, take a hard look in the mirror and, if necessary, do some adjusting on your end.

Tantrums are perfectly normal behavior for a child, but of course that doesn't make it easier for you to handle. Try to deal with it without anger and without submission. Here are our tips:

- *Remain calm.* It helps if you remind yourself that a tantrum is natural and not a bad reaction to frustration and anger. Use the Universal Strategy of ignoring from Chapter 2 to deal with the noise; go about your business if you can and wait for the storm to pass. If you're in a public setting, move your child to as secluded a spot as possible and simply stay with him or her until the tantrum subsides.

- *Don't show anger or disgust.* Your child is already going through quite an ordeal. Don't make it worse, because you will not be able to shame her into stopping.

- *Don't give in.* Don't let her do or get whatever caused the tantrum. Placating your child or giving in only reinforces the behavior and makes it more likely it'll happen again.

- *Don't try to reason with your child during the outburst.* Your child is a boiling sea of emotions and is in no frame of mind to listen to logic or reason.

- *Don't threaten punishment.* Saying something like "Stop it or I'll really give you something to cry about" is like pouring gasoline on a fire.

- *Name and validate your child's emotion.* When your child gets angry and loses control, say something like, "I understand you're really mad." Such a simple empathic acknowledgment teaches kids to communicate what they are feeling and lets them know that anger is not bad. They just need to learn better ways to express it.

- *Let the tantrum run its course.* Use the disengaging and ignoring strategies as they suit you best. If your child is really young, sitting down next to her, remaining calm but nearby, will be enough. For an older child, you might say something like, "I know you're angry, but you'll need to go to your room to finish crying." Or you can simply say firmly, "Go to your room to cool down."

- *Minimize physical interaction.* If it looks like a tantrum is turning physical, take your child to a place where he will do less harm. You can also use or create barriers to prevent him from lashing out. Don't let your child attack you or anyone else, or hurt himself, or destroy his or others' property. (See "Handle the Violent Tantrum" on page 73.)
- *Remember that your child is not an enemy.* Keep in mind that your child needs your help in learning mature ways of behaving. She needs to know that when she has lost control, you are there for her and will help her regain it. If you respond to her outburst with yelling or spanking, you lose the opportunity to be a role model for how to deal with upsetting feelings.

When the tantrum is over and your child calms down, it is time to begin rebuilding and positively reengaging. Wash her face and offer a drink of water. Let bygones be bygones and return to the positive relationship.

A quick conversation to reaffirm that there is nothing wrong or bad about feeling angry and a short request that the child talk about these feelings instead of having a tantrum, is appropriate. Don't drag your child back through the entire experience just when she has calmed down from it. Later on you can utilize the coaching and practice session strategies and refer back to this situation.

With older children, you might discuss what caused the outburst and how to resolve that specific issue. If together you can get to the root of the problem, you can help your child to find ways of expressing her anger more productively in the future. But again this should be a very short conversation that doesn't dwell on the incident.

Your key goals during your child's tantrum should be to avoid reinforcing the behavior; name her emotions for her; and offer up an acceptable alternative behavior, but leave the burden of calming down to her. You have to step in to educate your child and help her through the tantrum, but you shouldn't take responsibility for resolving her upset feel-

Children need to experience the cycle of calm-upset-calm.

ings every time she has them. Children need to experience the cycle of calm-upset-calm in order to learn how to manage themselves and their feelings. Be consistent with your child so that she knows what to expect from you during these episodes, which can be confusing to a child.

Note that the Universal Strategy of rewards is *not* one to implement if your child is having a tantrum. Any type of a reward, while it may stop the tantrum, will reinforce the behavior and you'll have more of them on your hands before long. Instead, use praise as soon as you see your child start calming down. You can even do this when he stops crying or screaming to take a breath. Use that lull in the noise to say, in a soft voice, "Oh, good, you're starting to calm down." This suggestive technique may deflate the tantrum right then and there. Afterward, praise the eventual return to calm. Finally, let go of any anger about the tantrum once your child starts to settle down, regardless of how upset it made you, so you don't make it start up again.

Use Coaching and Practice Session Strategies at the Grocery Store

What practically every parent immediately thinks of when it comes to his or her child having a temper tantrum is the grocery store. Rows and rows of every kind of food imaginable to a kid

> *There is so much that a child wants at a grocery store.*

are arranged in extremely attractive ways by grocery marketing geniuses. And then there are the checkout lines with candy and gum close to arm's reach. There is *so much* that a child wants at a grocery store, and limit after limit must be set. All of this becomes kindling for that dreaded tantrum.

A combination of the coaching and practice session strategies will help if your child is susceptible to tantrums at the grocery store. You can amend these to use in any other kind of public place that provokes your child, as well.

What follows are six steps for using the coaching and practice session strategies:

1. Choose a time for a practice session that is one in which you do *not* actually need groceries. You should not have any focus other than your child in order for these sessions to be effective.
2. Coach your child about what is expected, naming the kinds of behaviors the child has struggled with in the past. Include a discussion of what will happen if the child has trouble behaving (such as running off, tantrums caused by wanting something at checkout, etc.).
3. Take the actual trip. Go through the motions of a regular trip, all the while focusing on your child. Continue to provide coaching and intermittent reinforcement of appropriate behavior by giving specific praise such as, "I like the way you're walking right next to the cart instead of running off down the aisle!"

4. Be completely willing to go to a negative consequence, as discussed in Chapter 2, if things go south. This is the dreaded Time-Out in the store or leaving the store altogether despite a full grocery cart. (We've been there; it's *totally* effective but no fun at all.) This is why it's so important that this trip be only about practice and that you don't have any pressure to actually bring home groceries.
5. Be as polite as you can to the workers in the store, because they will be more likely to assist you if needed.
6. Afterward, make any adjustments required for the next practice session. Alternatively, it's okay to decide that your child really isn't ready and simply decide not to bring him to the store with you for the foreseeable future.

It's a cliché, but the tantrum at the grocery store is still as embarrassing and cringe-worthy for every parent to go through as it was for all the other shoppers in the store who had to go through it when their children were younger. Dr. Pete still recalls sitting on the floor in the aisle at the Tom Thumb grocery store, using the strategies outlined above and holding his tantrumming son, sweating and totally embarrassed.

Dr. Pete says, "What kept going through my mind was that if I follow through, then I'll have very few episodes like this, and if I don't, this will happen all the time. So I decided that if I was going to be this embarrassed, I'd better see a benefit to it."

Dr. Pete stuck to his guns, and the tantrums were few and far between. (Now his son is a college student who can control his temper very well.) Use your ignoring strategy with all the other shoppers in the store if you need to, and concentrate on helping your child through this tantrum.

Use Disengaging Strategy

If you have an emotional child, teetering on a tantrum, a short, empathic response to validate his feelings is worth a try. Simply saying, "I understand how you are feeling right now," in a nice, calm voice might just work. If it doesn't, move on to the disengagement strategy.

For children who are just trying to test you—perhaps she is stamping her feet or creating a fuss over something for which she knows better—the disengagement strategy will be especially helpful. When you're at home and your child has a meltdown, this option may also be your choice, as it can be relatively time-intensive. Since consistency throughout all of these strategies is necessary, make sure you don't have a schedule to keep to for the next hour or so.

You can disengage during a tantrum using the following approaches:

- Offer bland, automatic responses such as, "I understand that." This will allow you to reply to any tantrum verbalizations without reinforcing the behavior. Your child may test you for a while, but if you stick to it, most kids will get the hint.
- Don't feel that you have to justify the limits you are setting to your child or that you have to explain your reasons for whatever set off the tantrum. Those exchanges can be reinforcing to the tantrum.
- Give conditions under which you *will* discuss the situation with more than just an automatic response. For example: "When you've calmed down, then we can talk about why you don't like this rule."

- The less said, the better.
- Begin to busy yourself in a mundane task (like housework). This gives you a focus while your child calms down. Anything you say during a tantrum should be stated in a low, calm voice, which role-models what you want your child to do.

Understand the Violent Tantrums

There are some children whose tempers become violent during a tantrum. Sometimes kids will resort to hitting and kicking as they escalate the tantrum to gain parental attention. This can happen when you appropriately ignore your tantrumming child, and the child raises the stakes to get you to engage. This is fairly normal behavior, but that doesn't mean you have to allow it. If hitting is one of your Absolutes, and we'd encourage that it be on your list, do not under any circumstances allow your child to hit you or anyone during a tantrum. If you can physically control your child, then going straight to a Time-Out is appropriate for hitting. State, in a firm voice, "No hitting, time out!" and then institute a Time-Out immediately.

As your child gets bigger and stronger, however, this can be much more difficult. Even some 4-year-olds are too strong for their parents to control safely during a tantrum. Unfortunately, this situation presents a conundrum: You can't allow hitting, but it's really difficult to institute a punishment in the midst of a tantrum. It becomes a very messy situation.

So, your strategy needs to become one of damage control. Remove any other children from the area, and do what you can to not get hit: Use barriers, a couch, pillows, or whatever you can. Walk away if you have to; do it quietly so as not to add drama to the situation, but also quickly enough so that your child can-

> *Remember, the tantrum is all about attention.*

not chase you down. Remember, the tantrum is all about attention. You must separate yourself from your child, whether that means relocating the child or yourself. Once a situation escalates to this level, with a tantrum of this force, there is little you can do to stop it. You just need to let it run its course without letting your child hurt you, himself, or anyone else.

After it's over, it is appropriate to institute some negative consequences for hitting, especially if your child is older. Don't rehash the episode with your child in too much detail, but you and your spouse, or any other adult involved in the situation, need to examine the ABCs of what happened. Your goal is to control any contributing factors in the future to reduce the likelihood of similar events. Sometimes, the violent tantrums will happen again, even without the same triggers. This will be a learning process for you and your spouse, and you should start to see the occurrence of this level of tantrum decrease. If it doesn't, or you just feel out of your depth with these tantrums, Chapter 11 takes you through some indicators that may lead you to consider seeking professional help.

Reset a Negative Relationship

Too many escalated discipline problems, like violent behavior, can lead to feeling that you and your child have a negative relationship. If you feel that your relationship with your child has become a bit troubled, we'd like to suggest a reset before you move on to any other behavior shaping strategies in this book. These are strategies you can do from home. Wipe the slate clean, start from scratch, or at least flip the page to a blank one.

You can reset your relationship with your child using the following approaches:

- Make a list of your child's positive attributes—those characteristics that you enjoy about her. Actually write them down, and have your spouse or co-parent do the same.
- Think back to times when your child has been particularly helpful or displayed really good behavior. These don't need to be actions toward you, but include the way he treats his friends, teachers, other family members, or even pets. Add them to the list.
- Write down your child's top few traits that you find to be the most difficult to deal with, and then find a positive spin to put on each. For example, for a particularly stubborn kid, you might write down that she is confident in her opinions and shows strength in asserting herself. Learning to harness that passion and bring it under her own control will serve her well in the future.
- Commit to some Special Time together. This is actually a common clinical recommendation to help parents improve their relationship with their children. As often as daily or at least several times per week for 15 to 20 minutes, commit to being with your child and doing at-home activities together that are chosen by the child. Special Time is one-on-one: one parent at a time with one child at a time. Suspend judgment during this Special Time, and let your child direct the activity entirely. Special Time can be playing a game, going for a bike ride, or snuggling together before bedtime. Do not share any of your opinions about the activities chosen or the way the child is

Commit to Special Time together one-on-one.

acting. The idea is to create a regular time when your child is not worrying that he is going to get in trouble, and there is only positive interaction happening between you and your child. Do not break your promise about committing to Special Time, and do not allow this time to dissolve into yet another argument or you'll have put yourself so much farther behind in this process.

- Share the thoughts you wrote down about your child using the Universal Strategy of praise. Do this not all at once, but generally, and during conversations. Use those listed items via the praise strategy, even if the examples aren't necessarily recent. Find other reasons to praise your child as often as you can.

This reset is not automatic. It will take time. While you may have setbacks, continue adding to your list as often as you can. Make sure that both you and your spouse or co-partner acknowledges the fact that none of us is perfect: We all get mad and fly off the handle from time to time. Putting the time in with your child now will pay dividends in the long run.

• • •

Tantrums can mean a storm of arms and legs and screaming and crying, but if through it all you hold onto the fact that your child is expressing emotion in the only way he or she knows how, you'll be able to be more understanding of the spectacle. Knowing why this happens allows you to handle it in a stress-free manner, which in itself will help your child learn how to deal with these emotions in more positive ways.

Often the first foray into behavioral issues, tantrums are certainly dramatic but if you can approach them in the right ways, using our Universal Strategies and the tips outlined in this chapter, they should start to decline and be relatively short lived. Teaching your child how to more appropriately handle his or her emotions will help you avoid other behavior issues in the coming years and set the stage for continuing to build that positive parent–child relationship that is the basis for you both.

4

Homework

There's a reason why the word *homework* is usually uttered with a groan. Unless you're a kindergartner who's excited to be "old enough" to have homework, it's usually not much fun and akin to a chore. Think about it; when you get home from work, what's the very last thing you want to be doing? More work. Children feel the same way. It's unsurprising, then, when homework becomes a source of conflict and confrontation between you and your child.

From your perspective, doing well on homework leads to good grades, good grades lead to a good college, a good college leads to a good job, and a good job leads to good money and success in life. You are able to understand the future, abstract benefit that you do this for, but your child has no way to imagine the importance of choosing a college or future earning potential.

It can be easy to get too aggressive about making sure homework gets done and, in the process, lose sight of the need for your child to develop and practice the *skill* of doing homework, which is no different from any other complex skill he is learning in school. As with most aspects of parenting, helping your child improve at doing homework takes time, persistence, and consistency. There will be assignments that don't get done or turned in, and other little failures along the way. This is all part of the learning process and can lead to better homework habits when the stakes are higher.

As your child gets older (and homework gets harder), this source of behavior problems can become entrenched in your relationship with your child, so it needs to be dealt with at the earliest opportunity. Poor study habits, or allowing yourself to essentially do your children's homework for them because it's easier and faster, can become a difficult cycle to break unless it is caught early.

An irony we're sure is not lost on you when you are facing these issues is that most schools don't teach students how to do homework. They teach the subject matter, but often leave the study habits to you. From the first kindergarten worksheets on the alphabet to the square root of −4, homework is a skill that is acquired and developed over time—kids don't start school knowing how to do it. Complicating this situation is the fact that you might not even recognize the concepts your children bring home. Between nationally based curriculum and online high-stakes standardized testing, kids today are learning more at earlier ages and in more ways than ever before.

In this chapter, we help you understand your child's learning style, instill motivation for learning, and kickstart the process for helping your child work independently. We offer strategies for

> *Learning subject matter is great, but loving to learn is exponentially more powerful.*

making homework less painful for your kids and less stressful for you, with a special section for working with gifted children. It is crucial that your child not only develop good study habits, but also a good attitude about school and learning in general in order to be a successful student. Learning subject matter is great, but *loving to learn* is exponentially more powerful.

Understand Learning Styles

It will be helpful for you to understand your child's preferred learning style. Any time we are faced with the task of learning something new, the brain's learning and memory systems are activated. Each of us is wired to learn a little differently, and as a result we each have our own styles, some of which are more efficient than others. It's the efficiency of learning, the ability to learn the material well in the easiest way possible, that psychologists look at when they're working with a patient. A person doesn't learn exclusively one way, but by looking at how we feel most comfortable learning something new or acquiring a new skill we can deduce some of our learning preferences. By recognizing your children's preferences, you can play to their strengths when helping them learn.

While there are many models of how we process new information, there are three learning styles that are most frequently identified: *visual, auditory,* and *kinesthetic.*

Visual Learning

Visual learners need to see the teacher's body language and facial expression to fully understand the content of a lesson. They tend to prefer sitting at the front of the classroom to get the best view. They may think in pictures and learn best from visual displays, including diagrams, illustrated text books, videos, and handouts. During a test, they may remember their notes by actually visualizing them (for instance, where on the page a specific fact was written).

Auditory Learning

Auditory learners tend to learn best from verbal lectures, discussions, talking things through, and listening to what others have to say. They interpret the underlying meaning of information by understanding the words and concepts as described by language. Written information may have more impact if it is also heard. Auditory learners often benefit from reading text aloud, recording it, and then listening to the recording later.

Kinesthetic Learning

Kinesthetic learners tend to learn best through a hands-on approach, actively exploring the physical world around them. They want to handle something, touching or manipulating it in order to understand it. They often find it hard to sit still for long periods and may become distracted by their need for activity and exploration. However, when allowed to learn by doing, these individuals can be very efficient learners.

Instill a Motivation for Learning

Academic work in general is often not inherently interesting or motivating to many kids. Playing to their strengths and utilizing their learning styles helps a great deal with motivation, but you cannot simply expect that your child is naturally ambitious and driven in his schoolwork. Many kids aren't, and that is not ab-

Learning Styles: Approaches to Homework

It can be helpful for you to incorporate your child's preferred learning style into the way she does her homework. For example, if your child often has worksheets to complete, but has an auditory preference, you might have her read the questions out loud before she attempts to answer them. If your child is a kinesthetic learner, use manipulatives such as pennies for adding and subtracting, straws for grouping by tens, and so on. If she is a visual learner, teaching her to draw a chart of the subject matter will help with recall on a test.

All of this might not be feasible at the exact moment that she's doing her homework, but incorporating it later on that day or week will bring the subject matter to light in a new way and enhance her learning. Some teachers even flip their classroom, assigning listening or watching lectures as homework while they save the hands-on activities for in-class work, specifically to address the varied learning preferences of the class.

Most textbooks now have real-world examples, and you can find your own with a simple online search. That same search will likely pull up some visual learning options for your child, if that's his or her preference. To search properly, type in the learning style and the subject matter (for example, visual learner math). You can narrow your search by entering more specifics on the subject matter (such as visual learner multiplication tables), and find some very useful resources.

normal. This does not mean that they won't be ambitious or driven as an adult; when they are stimulated, you'll see the motivation kick in. Because kids see homework as taking time away from other activities that are way more fun and interesting, getting your children to do their homework involves teaching them a little self-sacrifice. Learning to put off something more enjoyable to do something that's necessary in order to reap the rewards later is a mindset that is crucial to their success as an adult with a job.

Getting your children to do their homework involves teaching them a little self-sacrifice.

One of the most important things you can do, regardless of your child's learning style or intrinsic motivation, is to instill a sense of curiosity and a value of learning during the preschool and elementary school years. This leads to a child who is motivated to learn new things. Without motivation, a learning preference won't make the difference.

Easy things you can do to foster curiosity and motivation are those same kinds of things involved in the strategy of cultivating a positive relationship with your children: Read to them, talk to them, spend time in new activities together, allow exploration without interference, and let them figure out themselves what to do with their time when they're bored. You can also help your child develop a motivation to do well in school by emphasizing its importance as well as working to develop your child's level of confidence and empowerment. You have to nurture your children's interests and talents even when they aren't aligned with your own.

When your children are old enough to read books on their own, continuing to read to them at night can be a fantastic way to nurture learning, cultivate that positive relationship, and cement a nighttime ritual. It can also expand their vocabulary and even get them interested in books of your choosing that they might not otherwise pick out on their own. Cooking with your child can be a STEM (science, technology, engineering, and math) lesson unto itself. Even Friday night pizza can be a way to sneak in some extra math, "Okay, Layla, the pizza's here, so why don't you put two-eighths of the pie on your plate, but give Daddy three-eighths!"

One of the best ways to instill motivation for learning is to specifically praise your child for sharing things she's learned. This helps her feel valued for what she knows and the process by which she knows it. For example, if your child shares a fact about dinosaurs, you can respond with specific praise that affirms the child's knowledge. You can also extend the conversation, which lets your child know that knowledge is important and valued, and this indirectly reinforces curiosity.

So, consider a different reply to that dinosaur fact than, "You're so smart!" A response that reinforces motivation for learning could be something like, "Wow! You know a lot about dinosaurs! Where did you learn that?"

You can continue showing interest and extending the conversation with, "Was that dinosaur a meat eater or a plant eater?" Keep in mind, however, that extending the conversation should never feel like a "test" to your child. He should go away feeling valued for his knowledge and curiosity, and even willing to go look for more information about the topic.

Similarly, if the child's interest continues, some extra steps that reinforce the same interest in learning might be checking out the dinosaur books at the library or a trip to the science museum on the weekend. Interests can come and go in children quite quickly, so if he doesn't want to take it as far as the museum, don't push it.

Establish a Process for Working Independently

The main goal of homework in general is to have children independently practice a skill they've already learned. The key phrase here is *independent practice*. Sometimes parents will tell kids when to do homework, where to do it, and how to do it. If, at every step of the way, you are there to prompt and prod (nag) until the next step is done, or if you fall into the common trap of doing the homework *for* your child, then he won't learn to work independently.

Homework is a habit, a routine. Habits take time and practice to develop, and early on unfamiliarity can lead to resistance. As your young child begins to get homework for the first time, you

> *Homework is a habit, a routine.*

should look at study skills as a developmental process that can take months to teach and years to refine. The investment of time pays off when your kids are older and the consequences of grades are much higher. In the big picture, an occasional incomplete or failed assignment in second or third grade will be far less meaningful than the missed or failed assignment in high school or college.

It may help to think about homework and independent practice as a three-step process: *organization, application,* and *completion.*

Organization

Being organized when it comes to homework is a way to manage many of the problems that can derail the process. Keep in mind that your young child is still learning the process of doing homework and may need guidance with organization. Being organized and learning to approach tasks in a systematic manner are invaluable. Let him have some input into organization whenever possible, though it is perfectly appropriate for parents to provide guidance. His sense of pride and ownership will be greater if he has a say in things like the selection of the desk organizers and colored folders he uses.

Establishing a routine is indispensable. Even something as simple as designating a place for the backpack to be left every day is part of establishing a homework routine. Your child comes in the door, and the backpack is left in the same place every day. There's no magic place; let her choose! If she puts it there, then follow with specific praise. If not, correct her by having her retrieve her backpack and move it to the agreed-on location. This begins the after-school routine and helps avoid the searching that sometimes delays and adds frustration to homework time. After homework is complete and assignments and materials are returned to the backpack, it is again placed in the same location so that it's easy to find the next morning.

Identifying a place where homework will be done every day is another starting point. Having the necessary supplies available is also essential. Again, these are both areas where you can let your child have a say, as long as her choice in location is relatively quiet and free from distractions. As always, you get the final say.

The time that homework is completed should also be part of the routine. This can be really hard for busy kids and busy families who are working around practice, game, and performance schedules. By prioritizing time for homework, you are sending the message that homework (in other words, school) is more important than any of those other activities.

Beyond that, you can provide guidance and allow your child some choices in terms of how to break their work down incrementally and put it in order. For example, if your child has several spelling words to copy and practice, a math worksheet to complete, a coloring activity, and 15 minutes of reading, you can help him identify each of these tasks. So instead of having to do "a lot" or "a little" homework, he knows he has four things to do.

Your child might make a sticky-note for each task, or a short checklist. Kids won't come up with these ideas themselves, so your guidance in establishing these kinds of organizational habits is helpful. Once the list is clear to your child, he may choose what he'd like to do first, and then next, and so on, and he can mark off each task in whatever way is quick and feels satisfying to him. Some elementary schools provide their own checklist in an agenda that needs to be signed each night or each week by a parent, so if that's the case, then simply make sure you and your child keep up with that.

You can also help your child identify natural break times in between tasks. This can stave off frustration and disinterest. Taken together, you're building the habit of an organized and systematic approach to homework that will help your child learn the benefits of self-management when doing any long or difficult task in the future. Your diligence and consistency now will enable you to back out of homework involvement later on.

Speaking of backing out, try not to be watching TV or doing some other fun activity that will take your child's attention away from what she needs to be doing or make her feel like she is missing out on something fun. You might take the opportunity to pay bills, do some paperwork, or read during homework time.

Application

Application is actually doing the homework itself and where much of the frustration kicks in. Many a child struggling with homework has gone to his mom or dad and said things like, "I can't do this," or "It's too hard." He then implicitly sits back and expects Mom or Dad to jump in and help him find the right answer. Frustration kicks in, and parents grumble but all too often are willing to offer the answer to the math problem or compose a sentence with the child's spelling word.

However, part of the point of homework is for your child to put what he's learned at school into practice on his own. The consistent message needs to be that you are available to help, but that help is specific and is not offered spontaneously.

In response to your child's blanket statement that she can't do the work, try to get her to ask a specific question. You can gently question your child back and in doing so help her narrow down the focus of what she's trying to figure out while still letting her figure it out on her own. Here are some questions you can ask in response:

- Which question are you on?
- Why don't you read the question out loud first?
- Which part don't you understand?
- What do you think you're supposed to do?
- The previous question can be followed with: Let me know when you have an idea. (Even a guess is okay if your child claims to have no clue.)

The idea with all these leading questions is to get your child to put forth some independent effort before you step in. Over time, if you're consistent, your child will learn that he needs to attempt the assignment or come up with specific questions when asking for help. He'll understand that the *I don't know*s and the *I can't*s won't lead anywhere.

> *The I don't knows and the I can'ts won't lead anywhere.*

With this approach, you're teaching problem-solving, which is a huge skill. Praise your child for any effort at figuring something out and then getting specific with her request for help. But don't go for the bland, "Good job!" Be specific with something like, "I can see you really thought about that and tried to figure it out—way to go! I can see how that part is hard, so let's see if I can help you understand it."

For some parents, the frustration in the application of homework is that we don't know how to help our children. Math has changed a great deal over the years since we were in school, as have many other subject matters. Even the youngest parents might not remember that long ago!

Online resources are a tremendous source of assistance here. Ask your child's teacher in the beginning of the year for a list of trusted websites where your child (you don't have to own up to this being for you!) can go to find additional information about the classwork. The online versions of textbooks often have video tutorials that break down each lesson. There are also plenty of teachers posting their own lessons online for anyone to view.

Completion

Once you've given some assistance and pointed your child in the right direction with the content, step away and let him complete the assignment on his own. For some kids, checking in with the parent after each completed task helps them keep focus—a high-five and some short, but specific praise here can go a long way in maintaining motivation for the next task.

Use of a *when/then* statement, as outlined in the giving good directions strategy in Chapter 2, is incredibly useful in helping kids muster the effort to complete homework. For example, offering a fun activity after homework is done can give a child something to look forward to: "When you finish your homework, do you want to play a game with me? Come and get me when you're done. I can't wait to play!"

> *Completion is first, correctness is second, and optimal performance is third.*

If he completes his homework independently but it is not quite perfect, offer to review it for him but *try not to impose*. It is important to look at homework as a developmental process: Completion is first, correctness is second, and optimal performance is third. Jumping ahead in that process too quickly tends to create resistance and frustration on the child's part. The idea is to praise and build the independent skill of doing his homework, not to overfocus on whether the homework is perfect. In fact, excessive review and correction can create such a negative tone for kids that they start to resist doing homework in the first place, which defeats the whole purpose. Many teachers rely on feedback from their students' homework to determine if they've mastered the concept, so forced perfection from home can make a teacher falsely think your child is ready to move on.

If your child is rushing through and technically completing the homework but putting forth little effort, then you might need to get more involved. A good place to begin is to contact the teacher about your concerns. It is, after all, the teacher's job to ensure that your child is learning the material, whether through homework or in class. A more extreme approach is to insist that your child do his own work and, if he suffers the natural consequences of a bad grade on the assignment, this should send a message. If the rushing through with no effort continues, you can start checking over the answers and offering some direction on which questions need additional work. Pushing children too hard for perfect homework scores can backfire and turn them off more than spur them forward, so you need to tread lightly.

Describe Homework at Your House

Choose the adjective that you and your child would use to describe homework at your house:

EASY   PRODUCTIVE   NEUTRAL   UNPLEASANT   TORTURE

Were your answers the same as your child's?   **YES   NO**

Why did you answer the way you did? _____

_____

_____

Did either of you choose the Torture answer?   **YES   NO**

If yes, what tactics have you used that have brought about the

most negative reactions from your child? _____

_____

_____

Do you see your child's resistance or negativity toward homework as:

INCREASING   STAYING THE SAME   DECREASING

What tactics could you use to make homework less

confrontational?_____

_____

_____

_____

Now, take the information you've learned in this exercise and request a parent/teacher conference. You don't have to get into all the details, but you can share with the teacher that you'd like to ensure that doing homework is a *positive* process for learning.

Use Positive Reinforcement

Using positive reinforcement is fundamental to your success in stressing the importance of homework. Recalling our ABCs from Chapter 1, the *consequence* is what happens after the behavior that makes it more or less likely that the behavior will occur again. Positive reinforcement will nudge that probability further along.

> *The praise strategy is a really basic but extremely critical.*

What you want to reinforce is that your child needs to work independently on her homework to its successful completion. The praise strategy is a really basic but extremely critical part of making it more likely that your child will successfully complete her homework.

Praise and rewards, both forms of positive reinforcement, will help you achieve this goal. Make sure that your praise is immediate, specific, and sincere and that your suggested reward is based on your child's completion of the specific task. Choose whether you want to reinforce your child's organizational skills, content comprehension, or assignment completion, and then build it right into your reaction: "I like how you sat right down and finished your homework tonight, without my even having to remind you! That means we have extra free time this evening. How would you like to play a board game, or go out for your favorite ice cream?"

The strategies of third-party praise and surprise both work well with homework and schoolwork issues. Let your child overhear you telling Grandma how hard she worked when she's selected to be in the school's spelling bee. Or, on a Friday morning after a long week with a heavy homework load, surprise your son with a trip to the donut shop before school for a special breakfast treat, letting him know how proud you are of his efforts and acknowledging that you know there are other things he'd rather be doing than homework.

Rewards also offer positive reinforcement of good consequences. As every teacher knows, a gold star or a happy-face stamp on an assignment is very motivating to many children. At its heart, this is purely acknowledgment that your child has worked hard on the task.

A homework chart, with rewards for good assignment completion either on a daily or a weekly basis, can be done both at school and at home. Your child can then see what he needs to do in order to earn up to the next goal. This is one of the best real-life applications of the regular interval rewards system discussed on page 49.

Just remember to be thoughtful in using rewards, making sure the good behavior happens first and then the reward comes into play: "After you finish that worksheet, we can play a game of checkers together." You can also stretch this out to use a larger incentive, such as getting a trip to her favorite restaurant after a whole week of doing homework on her own. There should always be something good that happens after homework is done, even if it's a high-five and a pat on the back most days.

Effect of Negative Consequences

Some students need to learn the importance of homework the hard way. Negative consequences reinforce against undesirable behaviors happening again. These can be strong deterrents. Try to resist the urge to bail your child out if he is unable or unwilling to complete his homework on time. The negative consequences

> *Natural consequences, potentially a late grade or a bad grade, can be a powerful lesson.*

that will occur in this case are also *natural* consequences, potentially a late grade or a bad grade, which can be a powerful lesson. It's much better for students to learn this lesson in elementary school than in later years when it can show on their permanent transcript. Remember, the goal is to develop homework skills over the long run, not necessarily to have *every* assignment complete and *every* answer correct.

Negative consequences can shape behavior when there's the need for a sharp turn. Here are two examples of applying negative consequences with homework:

1. "A big project due tomorrow, you say? It's too bad you didn't let me know sooner. The store closes early Sunday night, so we can't go get you a tri-fold board now. I guess you'll need to try to figure something out. Why don't you look around to see what you do have that you can use? Unfortunately, the directions say you need to present it on a tri-fold board, so I guess you'll lose some points right there."
2. "You don't want to do your homework tonight? Well, homework and school are important, so they have to come first. I guess since you don't want to do your homework, we can't go to your soccer practice. And you know, your coach says if you miss practice, you can't play in the game."

As stated in Chapter 2, negative consequences used in conjunction with praise can be very effective and powerful. Here's a tandem praise strategy for each of the above examples showing a follow-up. Each of these praises would be delivered by you a little while after the negative consequences took effect:

1. "You know, you waited too long before starting your project, and it's too bad we didn't have time to get a tri-fold board. But your teacher obviously thought your ideas were great, and so did I! I could tell you had thought about the project a lot. Next time, let us know you have a project to be working on, and we can make sure you have all the supplies you need to showcase those great ideas the right way."
2. "It's awesome your team won their game, and I hope next time you can be part of it. I know it was hard to miss a game, but you did a good job catching up with your homework and if you continue to work hard, you shouldn't miss another practice or game. Nice job, and I can't wait to see you play this weekend!"

Avoid Unintended Consequences

There are times when the best intentions for helping your child learn the subject matter and be able to do his homework have unintended consequences. Sometimes you are unaware of contributing factors that change the way your techniques work; other times the school gives parameters that rub your child the wrong way.

For instance, when it comes to a prescribed amount of reading for homework (some schools give guidelines such as 15 minutes of reading per night for first and second graders, and 30 minutes a night for third, fourth, and fifth graders), there can be some unintended negative consequences that sap motivation. As we know, reading is one of those crucial skills upon which all

Unintended negative consequences sap motivation.

other learning is based. From kindergarten to second grade, children are learning to read, and from then on they are reading to learn. It is critical that you take care to keep reading a positive experience for your child. While many schools feel they have to give a specific amount of reading, parents can and should be careful that it doesn't backfire. Mitigate what might become a negative experience by trying the following:

- Don't nickel-and-dime your child for every minute of their reading homework. For some children, setting a timer is very useful for engaging with reading, but with others it sets up reading as a chore and draws attention away from the book.
- Have plenty of high-interest reading material around and available. If your child is really into soccer or you're traveling somewhere this summer and he's excited about going, or if he just became fascinated with Komodo dragons, use that to motivate him.
- Count *any* kind of reading, including comic books, magazines, and even the sports page in a newspaper or website if your child is so inclined.
- Be a role model for reading by making sure your child sees you reading books, magazines, newspapers, and so forth.

Sports, clubs, and other outside activities are great for children and can enhance learning in many important ways. They also can be very motivating. But these activities may also be highly prized by your children, which makes them valuable targets for negative consequences. By keeping the focus on assignment completion more than on grades, you can make participation in out-side activities contingent on finishing their homework.

While this certainly will make your child sit up and take notice, if you are using this tactic you need to watch out for the unintended consequences. Take into account whether the exercise your child gets on the field will enhance his learning at home. Many times, children, especially those with high energy who have a hard time sitting still to do their homework, just need to get that energy out before they can concentrate on school-work. Playing a sport can be that release valve for them, and being part of a team will benefit their homework and grades in the long run. For kids who are not particularly strong students, out-side activities can provide an im-portant boost to their self-esteem and can be a safe haven from the beat down feeling they associate with academic studies. Consider

For kids who are not strong students, outside activities can boost their self-esteem.

your consequences carefully and always start with positive rein-forcement. If you do need to use a negative consequence, try not to take away more of an outside activity than is necessary and watch for unintended effects.

If your child needs constant supervision or guidance with his homework, that is a sign of a problem. He may have got used to lots of help from you, to the point where he cannot work inde-pendently. Here are some tips for dealing with this:

- See if there are after-care programs, tutorials, or study halls at school where your child can do his homework instead of bringing so much of it home to do evenings and on the week-end. This has the added benefit of taking the homework responsibility off your shoulders and avoiding battles over your child getting it done.

- Outsource homework oversight to someone else; often kids work a lot better for anyone other than a parent. Consider hiring a high school student or asking a trusted neighbor or relative, or even creating a homework study group with your child's best friend's family. Parents are often surprised at how efficiently their child works for someone other than themselves.

- Talk with your child's teachers and let them know what your child is doing at homework time, how long it is taking, and how much support you are providing. Especially for kids with special learning needs, there may need to be some adjustments in the amount of homework assigned and in the level of that homework. Talking to the teacher is the first step in getting the appropriate support.

- Check to make sure that fatigue is not a factor. Some children are able to do homework immediately when they get home from school while others may prefer to rest and begin homework after dinner. Yet others work best early in the morning before school. Experiment with different homework times and let your child have some input.

- Remember that your children may need to struggle a little in order to develop characteristics such as perseverance, independence, and self-confidence.

Work with Your Gifted Child

If you have a gifted child, you may not worry so much about homework, but you still need to be diligent. Your child may not have difficulty getting his or her homework done correctly and on time, and that's terrific, but when you consider the ABCs of behavior, there is a danger in reinforcing the wrong behavior of an exceptionally bright child. If your child doesn't have to work hard to get good grades, he or she may not develop a good work ethic.

Throughout this chapter, we've stressed the importance of effort rather than simply a good grade. This is true for students of all intellectual capabilities. Good grades can't be the be-all and end-all. It's easy to take your gifted children for granted early on, but simply telling them how smart they are and praising the good grades they earned with little effort is not going to meet all their needs.

It's crucial that you consistently impart the message that learning to work hard is what is valued. Gifted kids won't go far without a strong work ethic, so it should be specifically and deliberately emphasized as often as

> *Gifted kids won't go far without a strong work ethic.*

possible. Sooner or later, your gifted child will be challenged to succeed, and you need to teach her how to rise to that challenge. Teaching that now pays dividends in the long run, as her achievements will match her potential if she learns to work hard. An added benefit of helping your children rise to any challenge is that it will make their middle and high school years that much smoother.

Work out ways to challenge your gifted child. If she isn't getting enough in her classroom, make an appointment to speak with the guidance counselor and/or principal and share your concerns. Many schools now have online classes that can augment what's taught during the traditional school day, or offer classes in subjects (such as a foreign language) that may not be offered at your child's school. If your town has a local college, there are likely some resources there for gifted younger children.

•••

Now you have the strategies to use to help your children be successful with their homework. Remember, this is practice in the *skill* of doing homework, from organization to application to completion, which is no different from any other complex skill they are learning in school. Improvement comes from persistence and consistency over the long term. You understand learning styles and how to instill a motivation for learning, as well as a work ethic, which especially applies to gifted students who may not necessarily have a hard time with the content area on homework.

Throughout all homework issues and within the context of otherwise busy family schedules, all kids will need some downtime after school to relax and rejuvenate. When you're engaging in homework battles with your kids, the experience is not pleasant for anyone. If consistently negative, this can lead to school burnout, disinterest, and lack of motivation. Getting one night's worth of homework done is not worth diminishing interest in school in the long run or missing much of the next day due to exhaustion.

While homework offers teachers a way to measure whether their students have learned the concepts enough to practice them on their own, every child needs to have the opportunity to *love learning* something new. Elementary school is supposed to be exciting and fun, with new avenues opening up for your child in a variety of subject matters. Homework might not capture his imagination on a nightly basis, but it should not interfere with your child's academic performance in the future by adding to his negative perception of schoolwork. When your child is learning something that does get him excited, help him latch onto that excitement and follow it to its fruition.

5

Mealtime

*P*lenty of families struggle to manage behavior at the kitchen table. Siblings bicker, picky children complain about the menu choices, and we all wolf down our food in order to get to our next scheduled activity. You may find yourself fondly recalling the days of idyllic family mealtimes, with everyone sitting around the table, using their best manners, all happily eating the same freshly prepared food. For many of us, that may likely now be a rare occurrence rather than the norm. But it's understandable that frustration sets in when, inbetween volleyball games, dance recitals, kids complaining about the vegetables, and one or more parents working late, dinnertime doesn't work out the way you'd planned.

It's okay; idyllic may not be what you should strive for every night. We're advocates of setting *realistic* expectations for mealtimes and finding ways to enjoy stress-free meals with whichever members of your family happen to be home. Quality family

Regularly sharing time together with your children is what's important.

bonding time can take place at any meal, regardless of whether you're sitting around the table using the fancy china or standing up at the kitchen counter getting ready to dash back out the door as soon as everyone's done. Regularly sharing time together with your children is what's important; it's what facilitates communication, contributes to your positive relationship, and reduces problems.

Manage Mealtime Meltdowns

Peaceful meals begin with good preparation, and we're not just talking about planning menus and chopping vegetables. When it comes to the family kitchen, we go back to managing the series of contributing factors that lead to a behavioral problem. This is where you'll find the keys to being stress free. The goal is prevention of problems before they begin.

We have to do our part and role-model a good frame of mind by not adding to problems. This starts by not carrying stress from our day into mealtime. We're all rushed for time in trying to put dinner on the table after school or work, and that distress can easily carry over into lowered tolerance and less patience for our children.

In focusing on tantrums in Chapter 3, one of the first questions we advocated asking yourself was whether your child was hungry or overtired. A hungry child may be driven to distraction and display behavior problems more than a child who isn't hungry. This is more of a balancing act at mealtime, though, because you

Mealtime Stress Test

List the circumstances that contribute to stress at your mealtimes, and include everything that occurs to you.

Breakfast: _____

Lunch: _____

Dinner: _____

    Often, a purposeful slowing down of your pace can reduce the stress. Would you consider some sort of calming ritual to get yourself into a more peaceful mindset?   **YES   NO**

    What are some things you could do to ease your transitions? Some examples are waking up 10 minutes earlier in the morning, preparing ingredients for meals ahead of time, or decompressing on the couch for 10 minutes when you get home. (An occasional pre-dinner drink or glass of wine worked quite well for our parents' generation.)

_____

_____

_____

_____

_____

    Whatever you need to do to transition yourself into a more peaceful state of mind is worth the investment of time. As their role model, your kids take their cue from your behavior, and if you're at ease, they'll be more at ease.

> *Offer healthy snacks that literally fuel your child through his or her activities.*

want your children to be hungry when they sit down to it. But if they're "starving" for the half hour before, they're more likely to get into trouble. A light snack can help settle them down into your meal-time routine and tide them over without sapping their appetite.

Effectively managing mealtime is also a matter of good decision making about snacks and drinks throughout the day. Offering healthy snacks that literally fuel your child through his or her activities—school, extracurricular, playtime—works best for both nutrition and discipline. Limiting the empty calories of junk food and the caffeine in sodas goes a long way toward better behavior. Many parents have started planning for five light meals throughout the day instead of three larger ones, which only works if your child's school allows a snack time. This may work better for those children who are hungry all the time. Whatever the choices you make around your family's nutrition, use the Universal Strategies of role-modeling, giving good directions, and enforcing limits and rules to ensure that the lead-up to every meal is as positive and peaceful as possible.

Finally, you also need to manage distractions while your family eats. Keep the television off, don't answer the house or cell phone (it's most likely a sales call anyway), and institute a "no screens at the table" rule. Make sure *you* follow this rule as well as a good role-modeling strategy.

Establish a Mealtime Routine and Use Redirection

Like homework, engineering successful mealtimes is partly a matter of establishing routines and habits. Consistency of routine in general is a good behavior management strategy: Consistent routines are far less likely to provoke a behavioral issue than changes in routine. Children thrive on knowing what's coming next, and these years when they are young are the time for you to establish the habits that will last them through their lives. Eventually, a routine becomes ingrained into the brain of a child until it's simply second nature.

Your family may have busy schedules that make the "dinner at six o'clock every night" routine difficult. But it's not impossible to have a routine; you just have to find out how one works best for your family's schedule and situation.

One way to do this is to keep a family calendar of events. Variations on a schedule or absences of one parent or child can be anticipated so that mealtime doesn't dramatically differ from one day to the next. A general time frame of, for example, dinner between 6:15 and 6:45 can still become an established routine. If one parent works late every Wednesday, and Thursday is basketball practice, then the routine flexes to accommodate those weekly changes. After a few times, that flex itself becomes routine. It may make the most sense to update your calendar each year when school starts and then recalibrate as one extracurricular season ends and another begins. Some families find that reviewing the schedule on a weekly basis with their children allows everyone to be prepared as well as to provide input as to whether something has changed or can be managed differently.

And then there's the routine and habits of the meal itself. These serve double duty when it comes to discipline, offering both consistency and fodder for using the redirection strategy. Having a hungry child waiting to eat is a recipe for problems, so keep him busy in the lead-up to the meal. Involving your child gives him a sense of responsibility and an investment in the activity of mealtime.

> *A hungry child waiting to eat is a recipe for problems, so keep him busy.*

Begin by having him help with just one mealtime chore—the more regularly scheduled, the better. You can slowly add a chore every so often until a reasonable level is reached. Make sure that whatever duties you assign are developmentally appropriate (for example, some 7-year-olds can handle breakable dishes carefully, but others can't). Expecting a child to perform something unpleasant or uninteresting by himself may be asking for failure, so take some time to teach him how to do the chore successfully. Coaching and practice sessions are strategies that will help. Here are some suggested mealtime chores, by age level, that you can consider for your children:

- *Most 3-to-6-year-olds* can get out silverware, fold napkins, and put condiments (salad dressing, ketchup, salt and pepper) or other such items on the table.
- *Most 7-to-9-year-olds* can set the table, crack an egg, mix ingredients, and carry plates.
- *Most 10- and 11-year-olds* can cut up vegetables (always supervise knife use!), use the toaster/microwave, pour beverages, and do the dishes.

Let's say that your children need to clear the table after dinner. Be sure you give them good directions and role-model this behavior when they are younger and first learning it. This can also help to embed a natural incentive: Once the dinner plates are cleared, we can bring out dessert. A good cleanup routine for a family with multiple children assigns each a job. Eight year-old Diego brings the plates over to the sink, 10-year-old Cristina rinses them and puts them in the dishwasher, and little Isabella who's a preschooler, takes care of the cups. Keep the chores consistent and make sure they all understand that if one person isn't doing his or her job, it affects everyone: no dessert or TV time until the entire table is cleared.

If your family has mealtime traditions, such as saying Grace, you can involve your children by having each family member take turns at it. Selecting background music for your meal can be another rotating job, if it's something your family enjoys, but make sure to set parameters for those choices or you might end up with something that's not exactly conducive to a peaceful meal.

The last part of the routine can be very important from your child's perspective: the seating arrangement. Whether or not your family uses assigned seating, either formally or informally chosen, where a child is sitting can be of utmost importance. Siblings may need to be separated with a parent in between. One seat may be closer to something desirable, or be located in a less-advantageous spot than another, and this can cause competition. You can institute assigned seating at any time. However, a change in seating arrangements can also lead to behavior problems, so keep an eye out in this area.

Institute Rules and Use Reinforcement and Restitution

Hand in hand with mealtime routines are your family's rules. These can include basic table manners such as saying "please" and "thank you," sitting at the table until excused, and using utensils. Try to keep the list relatively short, because overwhelming children with too many requirements will be counterproductive. Use the coaching technique of reminding your children about rules they may have trouble remembering or sticking to during the time you're preparing the meal. Keep your tone instructive instead of fussy or corrective.

Here are a couple of examples of the coaching strategy regarding mealtime rules:

1. "Last night, I noticed that you were chewing your dinner with your mouth open. That's really not polite, and it's something I want you to try very hard to make sure you don't do. I'll remind you if I see you doing it today. I know you'll soon be able to remember this yourself."
2. "When you spilled your milk, I noticed you were trying to pass the salad to Mommy. I want to see you keep your cup further up on the table instead of right on the edge. Also, when someone asks you to pass him or her something, hand it to the person next to you who will pass it along. That's a lot safer and will help avoid another spill."

Eventually, your child will start to remember these rules. They will become habits, and you won't have to issue reminders.

Juxtaposed with your rules are those behaviors that you may decide to ignore, at least for the time being. Make your determination based on your child's age, of course, but the strategy of ignoring can be a good one to help keep the peace at the table. This strategy is based on the removal of reinforcing attention so that you don't inadvertently give your child a reason to repeat the behavior.

Pick your battles, and prioritize where you will spend your parenting energy.

You may choose to ignore little behaviors that can be annoying but are not against your rules per se. Pick your battles, and prioritize where you will spend your parenting energy and what you will ignore. A child talking a little too loud, mildly playing with his food, or being picky about making sure the different foods on the plate don't touch are all examples of behaviors that some parents choose to ignore at mealtime. Proactively pair your decision not to comment on these behaviors with the strategy of praise and positive attention when they talk in an appropriate voice, eat all their food without playing with it, and try a food even when it's touched another.

Praising your child for getting it right makes it more likely she will repeat that behavior. It also makes it obvious when you're ignoring something she's doing and makes the act of ignoring have meaning for your child.

Find behaviors to praise throughout the meal. Be specific in telling your children what you like seeing, so that your praise reinforces the exact behavior you want them to keep doing: talking nicely, waiting their turn, trying a new food, using their napkin, and saying "please" and "thank you." Even if mealtime has been a real problem in your family, if you look hard enough, you'll find opportunities to use praise.

> *Be specific, so that your praise reinforces the exact behavior you want them to keep doing.*

Looking for those opportunities means paying attention, which will help you continue to manage problem behavior triggers and step in with redirection when necessary. (The act of praising itself can be redirection if it causes one child to pay attention to something new instead of to what was bothering her.) Staying positively engaged with kids through ongoing attention and praise also helps reduce opportunity for provocation of a behavior problem.

Behaviors such as arguing or fighting with a sibling during the meal may mean you have to take your response up a notch. Some of these behaviors might overlap with your Absolutes, so you need to use your predetermined response. "There is no hitting in this family, Jason; you need to take a Time-Out. I'll set the timer for five minutes and when you're calm you can rejoin us at the table."

After the five minutes is up, and your child comes back to the table (assuming he's calm and ready to rejoin the group), you don't need to dwell on his problem behavior. Just have him apologize to the person he hit and then resume the meal as usual. If you have other children, use the Time-Out to explain that they don't need to escalate the situation any further.

For those times when all of your children are involved in an episode of bad behavior at the table, a negative consequence in which they all feel some discomfort or a natural consequence of apology and restitution is most effective. Here are two examples:

1. "You both just said some very mean things to each other, and that's not okay. I know you're hungry, but we're going to have to delay dinner now until your Time-Out is finished. Or can you both apologize to each other right now."
2. "Accidents happen. You need to get the paper towels to clean up, and I'll get the mop. Mac-'n'-cheese sure makes a big mess on the floor; we should all try to be more careful next time."

It goes without saying that messes are inevitable at mealtime. Accidents are going to happen, and sometimes often. Restitution in these cases means cleaning up, regardless of whether it was an act of bad behavior or an accident that caused the mess. Restitution is not a punishment; it's simply a natural consequence. While it may be inconvenient for your child and may motivate him to be more careful in the future, the main lesson you're teaching is that everyone cleans up a mess they have made.

Get Your Children to Eat New Foods

"I don't like that!"
"I want something else!"
"I won't eat it; I guess I'll just starve!"

We're guessing you've heard these phrases, or others like them, at mealtimes. Up until now, how have you responded? Going forward you should consider the context of ABC—antecedent, behavior, consequence—as it applies to these kinds of situations. Antecedents are those contributing influences that can lead up to a behavior. Behavior is what the child does. Consequence is what happens after the behavior that makes it more or less likely that it will happen again. Let's take a look at some scenarios.

Scenario One: Like many moms, Ada is trying to get her family to eat more vegetables. She decides to try green beans and makes a family recipe that she learned to love as a child. Both children take one look at what's on their plates and immediately express their disgust, loudly. Ada bristles because they are insulting her family recipe, they really need the extra nutrition, and they haven't even tasted it before deciding they don't like it. She tells them that vegetables are good for them and they'll just have to eat it.

Antecedent: Mom wants to try a new vegetable, but the kids don't like vegetables.

Behavior: The kids express disgust and demand something else to eat.

Consequence: Mom forces her kids to eat the green beans. They believe that Mom doesn't care about or listen to their feelings, and resent being forced to eat. This consequence reinforces their negative association with vegetables (possibly with new foods in general), but also reinforces mealtimes as an adversarial situation of Mom versus the kids. They are more likely to dislike vegetables in the future.

Scenario Two: Here's a tweak in the consequence. Ada, concerned about making sure her kids actually eat, switches midstream and fixes something she knows they'll eat even though it doesn't contain a vegetable.

Antecedent: Still the same.

Behavior: Still the same.

Consequence: Ada's children learn that complaining and demanding gets them what they want, which reinforces their behavior and makes it *more* likely they'll do it again. Her goal of broadening their palates is now farther away than it was 10 minutes ago, and she's set herself up to be a short-order cook, preparing different meals for the kids.

Scenario Three: Here's another twist. While Ada still bristles at her children's reaction to the green beans, she takes a deep breath, ignores the insult, and reminds them that the rule in their family is that they take a taste of everything on their plates.

Antecedent: Still the same.

Behavior: Each child takes a taste of the green beans. Neither pronounces the dish delicious, but the girl states to her brother, "It's not *so* bad." Ada's daughter has just reinforced the idea of trying new foods for both herself and her brother.

Consequence: Ada praises her children for trying the green beans, with some special attention to her daughter. Her children learn that they get praise when they try new foods, at least one child is on the path to potentially liking green beans, and it's *more* likely that they'll try the sweet potatoes Ada has planned for a dinner next week.

These simple scenarios will unfortunately not be the magic formula to getting your kids to eat more vegetables; the reality is there's no secret sauce for that. However, when you use your knowledge of the ABCs and apply them to eating behaviors, along with positive reinforcement efforts, you'll be on your way toward achieving your goals.

The fact is that kids don't like things that are unfamiliar. That's really at the core of a new-food resistance. Nutritionists will tell you that it can take offering a particular food anywhere from 12 to 20 times before your child learns to like it, but suggest you should keep trying so your child builds familiarity with that food. After a number of exposures, the food is no longer "new," your child is becoming accustomed to its taste, and his resistance is diminished. With the expectation that your child simply tries a new food, and using positive reinforcements and praise when he does, you're raising the odds that he'll learn to like the food sooner rather than later.

It can be frustrating, not to mention a waste of valuable time, to prepare something you know the kids won't eat. Remember the keys to keeping mealtimes stress free, and know that it's okay to

> *It can be frustrating to prepare something you know the kids won't eat.*

take shortcuts. Plan for your kids to only eat a bite or two, and prepare just a small amount of the new food for the adults at the table. You can even have a rule that your child must "try" a new food 15 times or so before expressing that he truly doesn't like it. Be a role model by eating and enjoying the new food. Only try a new food once a week or once a month if that makes it easier.

Think about your child's nutrition in terms of weekly intake instead of daily intake. This reduces the worry if they don't eat more than a tiny bite of a green bean on Wednesday but happily scarf down the broccoli with cheese sauce on Saturday. You might even solicit input from your children about what new foods to try. To do this, take a look at all the offerings at the grocery store and ask the produce manager to describe the tastes and origins of each. Additionally, you can ask your kids to poll their friends to find out their favorite veggies, and then put those into your rotation. If you really hit on something they just aren't going to like, perhaps then you consider allowing them to choose from a short list of substitutes in advance so you don't become that short-order cook we discussed.

When it comes to creating good eating habits in kids, there are a few *don't*s:

- *Don't force* your children to eat all of something they don't want to eat. While this crosses into nutritional and medical issues, from a behavioral perspective forcing it creates a negative association and can ultimately backfire into more eating refusal or, taken to the extreme, raise the risk for a serious health issue, such as an eating disorder. Positive reinforcement of good eating behaviors is what is effective in promoting healthy choices.
- *Don't shame* or criticize your child's food choices or weight. Even at the young ages we're discussing in this book, shame

cuts to the bone of a child's self-esteem and can cause more serious problems than not choosing the healthy food.

It's a parent's job to offer a healthy variety of foods, and it's a child's job to decide which to eat.

- *Don't indulge* a child's super-picky eating habits by catering exclusively to her whims or demands. It's a parent's job to offer a healthy variety of foods, and it's a child's job to decide which to eat. Continuing to offer everything the entire family is eating to a picky eater will *eventually*—it may take months or even years—allow them to grow out of their pickiness.

- *Don't worry* that your child will starve, vomit, or otherwise be put in danger if you don't feed them their favorite foods all the time. Kids eat when they're hungry. Talk with your pediatrician if you're really concerned, but once reassured, use your ignoring strategy for any of your child's dramatics. If he receives attention for reacting with a gagging reflex, then he'll act that out more often with foods he doesn't like, so ignore it. If he sees you get upset and fix him a different meal when he says he's starving, then he'll cry starvation all the more often.

Develop Strategies for Eating Out at Restaurants

Now that we've worked on some mealtime problems at home, and you know how to apply the ABCs to food-related behavior, it's time to take on one of the most difficult tasks known to parents: taking the kids out to eat at restaurants!

It's not really all that hard, but it certainly can be stressful. If even the thought of taking your kids to a restaurant stresses you out, try using the coaching and practice session strategies in advance to get your kids ready. You can try taking one child at a time to a restaurant at a non-busy time of day (try 2:00 P.M.), or even have fun playing restaurant at home, with your kids being the waiters and you taking on the role of your children at the restaurant.

Remember to be specific about what's going to happen: "We will sit at a table, and a waiter will come and take our drink orders first," and so on. Be sure to name or role-play the behaviors you want to see repeated, such as ordering with a *please* and *thank you*, not kicking under the table or banging on the back of the booth, and so on. One great real-world role-play idea is to print out the menu from the restaurant's website and have your child select which meal he or she will want to eat before you go.

Additionally, we've compiled these five tips for dining out that should help your family enjoy a stress-free meal:

1. *Choose the restaurant carefully.* Ask friends and family with children around the same ages as yours for recommendations of places they like. Check out the menu before you go in, and gauge the reactions of the staff to your children when you walk in. Don't be afraid to walk back out if you think this isn't the right place for your family.
2. *Bring your own activities, such as crayons and coloring books, if the restaurant won't have them on hand.* Most family-friendly restaurants will be ready with some of their own, though.
3. *Go for a walk around the restaurant.* Much of the fidgeting at restaurants is because children are curious about what's around them or are just feeling restless because they are confined to a table. Watch for warning signs of restlessness and use a redirection, such as washing hands in the bathroom, as

a reason to move around. Also, a perimeter walk can satisfy their curiosity, give them something to talk about during the meal, and serve as an incentive for good behavior throughout the meal. "If you can follow the rules for good behavior in restaurants, we can walk over again to see the fish tank by the hostess stand on our way out."

4. *Give your child a job to do, such as reading over the menu on her own to choose her meal.* This helps to manage problems before they start and also helps children to practice their *pleases*, *thank yous* and reading skills.

5. *Ask for your children's food to be brought out first.* This cuts down on their filling up on the free bread and then not eating the main course and also reduces their wait time. When the adults are eating their main course, your children can be served desserts.

All of these steps help you establish a "restaurant routine" for your child, and once they're familiar with it, dining out becomes a more enjoyable experience for everyone. But even if you follow all these tips, some children are just going to experience a meltdown at a restaurant. If that happens to you, follow the same steps we outlined on page 70 in Chapter 3, substituting "restaurant" for "grocery store." It's also okay to hire a sitter and go out without your kids, especially if you know you're going to a place where you'd anticipate a meltdown or problem. Just because we're parents doesn't mean we're obligated to bring our children everywhere.

It's okay to hire a sitter and go out without your kids.

• • •

Above all, meals should be a pleasant experience, wherever you're eating. With a few of the suggestions in this chapter you can make your family's meals both healthy and peaceful and teach your children some of the important manners having to do with eating. All of this will serve them well as they mature and start having opportunities to eat at friends' houses or go out to eat with other families or groups.

6

Bedtime

*A*t the end of the evening, just as you're winding down and starting to relax, do behavior problems begin to erupt? Sometimes it seems like it never fails; at the very moment you're feeling that you are home free, a problem crops up unexpectedly and puts a damper on the evening. Unfortunately, bedtime is ripe for difficult behavior.

Forgotten school projects are suddenly remembered. Sibling rivalry kicks into high gear. Tantrums arise. Resistance is high. Stress levels skyrocket. And then there are the many entreaties that kids make as the lights go off and the blankets are tucked in that can exacerbate or restart the problems and the drama.

Bedtime should be a period of relaxation and winding down after a long day. Calmness should make the transition to sleep an easy one. But in a home with children, you know from experience that it's not always like this.

Luckily, bedtime is one of those problem areas over which you have a bit more control. This is a parenting issue that you can manage very effectively by using our Universal Strategies consistently, calmly, and, in some cases, creatively. The creativity comes in because routines and traditions play a big role in reducing the stress and problems at bedtime. They also provide an opportunity for you to strengthen your bond with your children as you soothe them. Putting your own, unique spin on these strategies is critical and can be very effective.

Think back to your own childhood. How do you remember bedtime—calm or chaotic? What comforted you most? Perhaps your parents sang special songs or read special books. Maybe there was a stuffed animal or pillow that made going to sleep more comfortable. While many of these soothing techniques begin when your children are very little, it's never too late to implement some new routines or introduce treasured traditions to the next generation.

In this chapter, we look at the importance of sleep and the causes of bedtime problems. Then we go through some of the best Universal Strategies that will help make your nights go more smoothly. Additionally, we examine how to soothe your child after a nightmare. As with all things related to raising your kids, you have to first understand the root cause of the problems before you can fix them. Knowledge is often the best stress relief there is.

Your Child's Sleep Is Very Important

Research indicates a strong link between the quality and amount of children's sleep and their cognitive, academic, behavioral, emotional, and health outcomes. A full range of difficulties have been associated with insufficient and poor-quality sleep, including lower performance on IQ tests, poorer performance on classroom tests, and lower grades in school. Poor sleep is also associated with behavioral problems and trouble regulating emotions and mood. Studies have found that children

Sleep nourishes the brain, similar to the way food nourishes the body.

whose parents do not enforce a regular bedtime are at greater risk for health problems. Additional research indicates that families that use a bedtime routine have children who tend to fall asleep faster.

Sleep nourishes the brain, similar to the way food nourishes the body. Those of us who either occasionally or routinely do not get enough sleep can certainly relate to the negative effects.

Not getting enough sleep can be behind health problems that are seemingly unrelated. It's not common, but the following scenario has happened: A child with undetected sleep apnea is tired and unable to focus in school and is diagnosed with ADHD. At some point, he has his adenoids and tonsils removed (which fixes the sleep apnea) and the ADHD goes away because he's now getting enough sleep. Doctors then realize the symptoms are stemming from the apnea and that the boy may never have had ADHD at all. While this is a scary possibility, we're sharing it to underscore the point that not getting enough sleep can have major ramifications.

One question that parents often have is how much sleep their child needs. The National Sleep Foundation recommends that preschoolers typically get between 11 and 13 hours of sleep a night, that children in elementary school get between 10 and 11 hours of sleep a night, and that teenagers get an average of nine-and-a-quarter hours of sleep a night. The organization is quick to point out, however, that these are rules of thumb, and that each individual has his or her own sleep needs that can be determined only by assessing how the individual feels after different amounts of sleep. Most children stop napping by 5 or 6 years old, so if your school-age child seems tired enough during the day to want to nap, this may be a sign that he or she is not getting enough sleep at night.

As we've already established, a child can have a hard time putting his or her feelings into words, and this often translates into tantrums or other problematic behaviors. Children don't know they're tired, and certainly would never admit to it. You need to observe your child and his or her sleep needs closely. Even within a single family, one child may be able to function normally and happily on 9 hours of sleep a night, while the other is cranky unless he gets 11 hours of shut-eye nightly.

Regular exercise can have a positive impact on sleep patterns. Engaging in vigorous daily activity, whether it's an organized sport, a brisk walk with Mom or Dad, or an hour at the playground after school, helps bedtime matters in measurable ways as well. That's not to mention how healthy it is for us all to be active rather than sedentary.

Bedtime can become a battle of wills between parents and children, and you may often not know where to turn to help your child achieve regular sleep patterns. You may resort to strategies such as keeping your child up extra late in order to tire her or him out more, but that tactic only backfires and makes the problem worse. Circadian rhythms have dips and rises and, just like adults, some children get a second wind of energy in the evening hours. This can make it appear that your child is not tired, but in reality she's likely to be *overtired*. If your

Keeping your child up late in order to tire her out only backfires.

house experiences what some parents (including Sara) call "the witching hour" between 6:30 P.M. and 8:30 P.M., when more behavior issues erupt, then circadian rhythms may be at work.

Additionally, children become adept at delay tactics such as asking repeated questions or last-minute requests for snacks and drinks, which can push a parent into frustration and push the situation into a problem. A child may say:

- "I'm still hungry"—after a full dinner with second helpings
- "I'm still thirsty"—even after a third drink of water
- "I can't fall asleep"—within the first two minutes of lying down
- "I'm scared"—saved for the last plea, said in a whisper while her hands clutch at you to prevent you from leaving the room

All of these may be valid requests and concerns. The child may still be thirsty, and many children, of all ages, are scared at bedtime. Your challenge is to enforce limits while maintaining a tranquil setting that's conducive to sleep. This is not an easy task, but by utilizing our Universal Strategies, you'll be able to work your way into a better bedtime and all the benefits that brings to your family.

Use Universal Strategies for Bedtime

One of the hardest parts of enforcing a regular bedtime is that you may feel tired yourself and simply want to wind down and relax rather than fuss over your child who resists going to bed. But a short-term investment into establishing healthy and regular sleep habits will earn you a long-term payoff in a child who goes to bed more easily. Once accomplished, you can end up enjoying more downtime after his bedtime because you put in the

A short-term investment into establishing regular sleep habits will earn a long-term payoff.

effort to help him establish good sleep routines.

The goal with the following strategies is to establish a set of cues that are associated with sleep onset. It's like setting a reminder in your child's brain that says it's time to sleep, just like sitting down to a full plate of food tells your brain it's time to eat. The consistency of routines helps to establish this association between a particular set of cues (bedtime routine and rituals) and falling asleep, so your child will start to *expect* to sleep when the bedtime routine is initiated. It's a cyclical process: The routine itself facilitates sleep onset by creating a calming environment in which falling asleep is easier to do.

While it's great to start from the time they're babies, good bedtime routines can be established at any age. Just a few tweaks that result in even 15 minutes of extra sleep a night can make a

Even 15 minutes of extra sleep a night can make a real difference.

real difference, so an incremental transition will be the best approach. Using the Universal Strategies with applications specific to bedtime, as outlined ahead, will help your child enjoy the full benefits of adequate sleep.

Cultivate a Positive Relationship

Cultivating a positive relationship is useful for every situation, but it's extra special at bedtime. A child who feels secure and content at home is a child who will be able to settle down a little easier when it's time to go to sleep. When he feels comfortable sharing his fears, the very act of talking about them may alleviate the worry and allow him to fall asleep without as many issues. Please don't misunderstand us: A child who has a great relationship with his parents may still have fears and problems falling asleep. It's just that those who don't have that positive relationship may have more trouble doing so.

The concept of a "clean slate" is another piece of the positive relationship strategy that is crucial to pacifying problems. A child who's been in trouble a great deal, but knows that when she wakes up in the morning she'll be starting anew, will feel much better about the end of the day and refreshing herself with sleep.

Engage in Role-Modeling

When it's nearing bedtime, the entire household should begin to wind down. Some children have difficulty falling asleep when they believe that siblings or parents are still awake and doing fun things. Particularly for children who are resistant to going to bed, it's important that your household environment begin to calm down as bedtime nears, because this can assist with your child settling in to sleep more easily. If you have older children who aren't actually going to sleep right then, they should stay quiet in their own room or another part of the house. Any media viewing should not be audible or visible to your child going to sleep.

Enforce Limits and Rules

Here's the crux of the bedtime solution: You need to thoroughly explain all limits and rules to your children in advance of the situation in which those limits and rules need to be enforced. And then the enforcement must be consistent.

Consistency dictates how fast children learn, and consistency is especially fundamental when you're dealing with bedtime problems. When it comes to bedtime, consistency means repetition. Kids will try all kinds of tactics to get out of going to bed or staying in bed, so you need to be ready to respond consistently every time. Be rote and repetitive, disengaging from any drama your child may attempt to incite. Each time your child gets up, lead him back to bed. Each time he calls out for you, simply respond, "I love you, it's time to go to sleep now."

Here are some tips for enforcing limits and rules:

- Bedtime is not the time to institute a new rule. Have a discussion at breakfast and then again during dinner about any new guidelines you're putting in place so that your child has enough time to process them. Consider introducing the new rule on a Sunday, so that you start the week out on the right foot. If it's a big rule, choose a landmark date so your child is prepared well in advance. Alternatively for major changes, just prior to the start of the school year is a natural date to start a new routine.
- Maintain a regular wakeup time and bedtime, particularly if your child is having trouble going to sleep or waking up. Unfortunately for those of us who like to sleep late on weekends, these should be enforced seven days a week. (As your child gets older, or after the schedule has been in place for a long while, he or she may not require such a rigid schedule and you can start to be a bit flexible on weekends.)
- Don't try to use weekends to get your kids "caught up" on their sleep—this is a myth. When a child has very different sleep/wake patterns during different times of the week, this increases the likelihood for insomnia during the week and results in greater difficulty falling asleep on school nights, kind of like permanent jet lag.
- Sleep experts universally agree that a standard bedtime routine can help promote a relatively easy and quick transition to

sleep. One example includes a bath or shower, brushing teeth, and then 30 to 60 minutes of quiet activities before bedtime, such as reading or listening to a story before lights out. This is where you can be creative and hearken back to your own youth for calming ideas.

- Sleep experts also discourage watching television, using video games, or engaging in vigorous exercise as bedtime nears. When the brain is highly stimulated by these types of activities, it takes longer to transition to calm and to sleep. It's for this reason that every child development expert advises us to keep screens out of the bedroom. By the time they're adults, they'll be able to self-regulate screen time, but at this age they can't.

- A light snack/drink an hour or two before bedtime might help to satisfy hunger. Just make sure it doesn't contain caffeine. One of those small medicine cups in the bathroom for bedtime drinks will allow them to wet their mouths without filling their bladders.

- For kids who truly are anxious about going to sleep, a common preemptive strategy can be the "Get-Out-of-Bed pass." The pass can be used only once a night to get a drink, or briefly talk to you, or for anything your child needs. This gives him a sense of control and some power in managing his fears, because it lets him know that if his fears get bad enough, he has a plan.

Redirect Focus to a Specific Task

In most cases, you can gently redirect your child to the task at hand, settling down and getting ready for bed. Use those *when/then* statements: "When you finish brushing your teeth and you're in bed, I can start the story." Be sensitive in your redirection, especially as it pertains to your child sharing her fears with you, so that you still validate her feelings before you try to get her to focus on something else: "I know you're a little scared, but Mommy and Daddy and (name pets, anything that makes them feel secure) are right here protecting you every minute. Let's see . . . which stuffed animal do you want with you tonight?"

Coach for Specific Behaviors

Coaching is a terrific strategy with bedtime problems because it allows you to be there for your child when needed, but at the same time express confidence that he can do it independently. Remember to be very specific in naming the behaviors you want to see, specifically the routine you've set up for your family. Give reminders throughout the process: "Didn't that shower feel good? Now, dry yourself off and then it's time to brush your teeth."

Periodic check-ins can be a form of coaching, too. Tell your child you'll check on him every so often if he stays in bed. These check-ins can be spread out over longer time intervals, and eventually phased out altogether as he grows accustomed to the bedtime routine. But know that if you say you're going to check in, you need to follow through. Nothing will mess up trust and provoke fear like a broken promise. If you're consistent with check-ins, you'll find that your child will start falling asleep more quickly.

If you say you're going to check in, you need to follow through.

Practice Bedtime Routines

It may seem a bit contrived to practice going to bed, and for some children, especially older ones, it will be. But the point that you make by doing a practice session with your child about bedtime routines is that this is important and that your child doesn't currently do it well. So pick a time when she's happy, compliant, and when it's still light outside so her fears are not an issue. Show her how you want her to do it (going through all the steps of the routine, including having her hop under the covers for even five seconds), and then you both have an experience to reflect back on when you're going through the real thing. Throughout coaching and practice sessions, remember to use praise.

Offer Praise and Positive Reinforcement

Praise and positive reinforcement should be used liberally throughout all the strategies involved in bedtime behavior. Be specific, sincere, and build on your successes: "I liked the way you got right into bed last night and listened to the story. You're doing a great job! Let's get you one last drink of water now, because I noticed how many times you asked for a drink of water last night, and then it's time to go to sleep."

You can even use praise as a preemptive strike against your child getting out of bed again. Wait a minute or two after putting him to bed, and then go back in and praise him for remaining in bed. That positive attention will reinforce the behavior you want to see: staying in bed.

Use praise as a preemptive strike against getting out of bed.

Use Disengaging and Ignoring

You may need to implement the disengaging and ignoring strategies during those times when you need to set a limit, but because bedtime needs to remain a placid experience, you really don't want to institute a negative consequence. Disengaging means you give a neutral, superficial response that does not feed into the heightened emotions of bedtime. An automatic response to those endless requests for another hug or announcements of being scared, repeated in a quiet, calm voice, can keep the focus on the matter at hand: "I know, but it's time to go to sleep now."

Similarly, if your child gets out of bed, you *must* take her back to bed as many times as it takes, ignoring the inevitable pleas for attention, all the while staying calm and having as little reaction as possible. Some children will really push this, especially if it's worked for them before, getting out of bed 10, 20, or even 50 times to test your response. Repetition, serenity, and consistency are what will combat this behavior. If she meets with the same response every single time she gets out of bed, eventually (sometimes it takes several nights) she'll stop trying.

> *Any extra attention will reinforce the behavior of getting up, especially if you give in after the 50th time.*

It's really hard for us to stay disengaged when this happens. But any bit of extra attention will reinforce the behavior of getting up, especially if you give in after the fiftieth time. That's when they know they can wear you down, so the next night it might be a hundred times. Take turns with your spouse if you can. Perhaps begin on a night when you don't have to get up early the next morning. Stay strong, disengaged, and calm.

Contend with Childhood Nightmares

A frequent culprit in the cause of bedtime anxieties can stem from childhood nightmares. These are bad dreams that most often occur during REM sleep. Nightmares can start in children between ages three and six, but they can happen at any age. The occasional nightmare is normal and not a cause for alarm, beyond the need to soothe your child back to sleep.

Repeated nightmares can have ramifications for your bedtime routine, feeding your child's fear of going to bed or fear of sleeping alone. Of course, the sleep disturbance for both parent and child will also have an effect on behavior the next day.

Typically, a child is able to recount the events of a nightmare, which often involve some type of threat to him or his security. If your child wants to talk about the nightmare right then, let him, but don't prolong the conversation with questions or a drawn-out discussion. Allow him to get his feelings off his chest, and then save your conversation for the next day, if at all.

If your child wants to talk about the nightmare let him, but don't prolong the conversation.

Children who have the occasional nightmare need comfort and reassurance. Dr. Pete advocates staying with your child until she or he is back to sleep rather than bringing your child into bed with you. Bringing him or her into your bed can become a recurring habit that can be difficult to break, and you should consider whether that could be a problem for you.

There's no wrong or right answer here, as long as you're intentional about your choice and think it through. Sara elected to bring the kids into her bed, which began a years-long habit, but she was able to institute limits that worked for her children and husband. Her rules: Everyone had to start the night in their own bed, but in the middle of the night, if the kids needed to come in, they could. Eventually, her children weaned themselves off this habit on their own.

Nightmares may occur or increase during or following stressful periods for kids. Common times are major transitions, like back to school in the fall, before a big test, or after the death of a family member. If the nightmares are stemming in part from stress or anxiety, the source of the stress needs to be identified, and methods for changing this and/or coping with this need to be put in place.

If your child experiences occasional nightmares, you can use the coaching strategy to help her through it and to get past the memory for the next bedtime(s). It may be helpful to share with her an experience that you've had with a nightmare, to show her that everyone gets them every once in a while and that they aren't real, no matter how real they feel.

Nightmares need to be differentiated from *night terrors*, sometimes called *sleep terrors*. These occur during non-REM sleep, and typically a child screams and seems terrified for a few minutes before falling back to sleep. The child is confused, doesn't recognize the parent or caregiver, and is not consciously awake. Unlike a nightmare, the next morning kids don't remember having a night terror at all, although it's always memorable for a parent. As scary as they are for parents, in and of themselves, the presence of night terrors is not necessarily the sign of a problem.

If a child is having recurrent night terrors or nightmares to the point of disruption for child and family, professional help should be sought. Talk to your family's pediatrician about the problem. Sometimes they may refer your child for a sleep study or to a mental health professional to address anxiety/stress symptoms and methods of coping. We go through the signs that indicate you may need professional advice in Chapter 11.

• • •

In using the strategies in this chapter, you should absolutely incorporate your own take on soothing children at bedtime. Make the routine a special time for your family. While cultivating a positive relationship can help make bedtime easier, a good bedtime routine can also nurture that relationship. And though your children may not love the rules you institute, that structure will help them settle in for the night, and they'll come to rely on them as part of the routine.

When traveling and staying overnight either at Grandma's or a hotel, consider ways you can keep to the bedtime routine, within reason. For some kids, having their favorite scented bath bubbles or making sure they have their blanket, stuffed animal, or pillow may be helpful in translating bedtime to a new place. It's not necessary to replicate the entire routine like a Hollywood soundstage, but an element or two can help cue your child and anchor him to the bedtime routine he's accustomed to at home.

When dealing with problem behaviors at bedtime, try to remain calm and use a soothing voice, which will reinforce the idea of settling down. Above all, remember that your children can be comforted best by you, the person who cares most about them in the world.

7

Attitude

There may be nothing as likely to push our hot buttons as a set of rolled eyes and a sassy retort of "Whatever!" from our offspring. It's frustrating, maddening, exasperating, galling, vexing—you know what it feels like. But as obnoxious as it can be, it's also completely normal behavior.

Attitude is a child's way of starting to show independence. She isn't ready to break off from parents in meaningful ways just yet, but she is asserting control over that which she has the means to control at this age: her tone of voice, her facial reactions, and her physical proximity to you.

So, she'll pull her hand away when you're walking across the street together. He'll grumble under his breath in response to chores or corrections in behavior (and perhaps even utter a curse word he's heard). He'll shy away from public hugs and kisses, and may ask you to drop him at the corner or just by the door when going visiting. "Mommy and Daddy" will become "Mom and Dad," and you'll realize they'd rather be with their friends than with you.

These can be bittersweet transitions for parents; your baby is growing up and it seems like it's going so fast. Continue cultivating that solid foundation of a positive relationship every chance you get, and remember that deep down underneath this new exterior are children who still need you and want you in their lives. They just might not admit to it.

In this chapter, we discuss those attitudes you may encounter from your children. Where do they come from, why are they so frustrating, and how can you best handle them? Just remember your ABCs—antecedent, behavior, consequence—when you're dealing with attitude.

Contend with Hot-Button Behaviors and Judgment Calls

The first order of business is for you, along with a spouse or co-parent, to determine your hot-button behaviors. These are those attitude behaviors that just make your blood boil when you see them in your child. They get under your skin, and you feel a reaction is necessary.

But while you may *want* to react, you need to think about *whether* you should react. Dealing with attitude behaviors is all about choosing your battles. You have limited time and energy to expend on parenting, and you need to determine if these hot-button behaviors are worth your effort. There's *no* rule that says you have to intervene in order to be a good parent.

While you may want to react, think about whether you should react.

Just what those hot-button behaviors are differs from individual to individual. Even spouses may have very different hot buttons, which can result in inconsistent parental reactions and sow the seeds of confusion, frustration, and sometimes even resentment by one spouse toward the other. It's important to know your hot buttons and your spouse's, and to either discuss or at least take cues from each other in determining your responses to your kids' attitude behaviors.

Knowing which attitude behaviors get under your skin is just an extension of the strategy of prioritizing your absolutes. While these kinds of behaviors don't rise to the level of an Absolute, such as hitting or biting might, the process for determining how you're going to react is similar. If you decide that you can't allow a particular behavior, then you need to settle on a reaction that you'll take consistently *every* time you see it.

Making judgment calls is part of what causes a parent stress. When dealing with behavior, judgment calls are the more difficult parenting decisions. It's hard to know what the right call is in many situations. The good news is that there's no absolutely right answer, though some decisions are easier than others. When your child hits, it's easy to know that's not okay and you draw the line appropriately—no hitting. With attitude behaviors, the line can blur because there's no universally right or wrong calls for you to make. When it comes to attitude, you get to decide which behaviors you want to correct and which you're willing to let go for now. In that sense, you have options—to intervene or not, to spend energy on a behavior or not.

Judgment calls are value laden. You need to implement your own value system in determining your reaction, along with consideration for the values of your spouse, grandparent, or other adults in your child's life. Consider *why* you react the way you do and perhaps you'll find some clues to help you change your own reactions. We all have limited energy resources to deal with child behavior. We can't intervene for every little thing or we'll exhaust ourselves and end up parenting in an inconsistent manner.

Table 7-1 is a chart of some of the most common attitude behaviors in kids between the ages of 3 and 11. This isn't a comprehensive list, because kids will always come up with creative ways to show attitude, among other things, so there's room at the bottom for you to add those other types of behaviors you see. Go through this list with your spouse or co-parent and rate them. Mark 5 for your strongest hot-button behaviors and make 1 represent those that don't bother you that much. There's also room for another adult who spends a good deal of time with your child, perhaps a grandparent or childcare provider, to note their hot-button behaviors on this chart.

Table 7-1 Attitude Behaviors Chart

Behavior	Your Rating	Co-Parent	Other Adult
Eye-roll	1 2 3 4 5	1 2 3 4 5	1 2 3 4 5
Backtalk	1 2 3 4 5	1 2 3 4 5	1 2 3 4 5
Sarcasm/smart aleck comments	1 2 3 4 5	1 2 3 4 5	1 2 3 4 5
Denial of responsibility	1 2 3 4 5	1 2 3 4 5	1 2 3 4 5
Dismissive tone	1 2 3 4 5	1 2 3 4 5	1 2 3 4 5
Constant arguing	1 2 3 4 5	1 2 3 4 5	1 2 3 4 5
Foul language	1 2 3 4 5	1 2 3 4 5	1 2 3 4 5
_____	1 2 3 4 5	1 2 3 4 5	1 2 3 4 5
_____	1 2 3 4 5	1 2 3 4 5	1 2 3 4 5
_____	1 2 3 4 5	1 2 3 4 5	1 2 3 4 5

Is cursing tantamount to blasphemy in your family? Does lying rise to a higher level of transgression for your spouse? When your child sasses you, do you consider it defiance and insubordination? Do either of you interpret the eye-roll as a lack of respect? Now is the time to have a mindful discussion of the *reasons* for each of your answers with your spouse or co-parent.

For any of these behaviors that you both (or all) rated a 2 or lower, see if you can come to a consensus to simply let those annoying behaviors go. In the scheme of things, they fall so low on your priority list that they literally aren't worth your energy or focus.

Try to agree on a framework for your shared values, taking into consideration each of your hot-button behaviors. Your goal is to cut down on inconsistency among those parenting your child. Determine if there are any behaviors that are low priority, and then let them pass by without reaction, paying them no attention. A framework doesn't mean you have to do everything the same way, however. Understand that in the heat of the moment, or based on circumstances, you may have to tweak your agreed-upon responses, but your framework should help to direct you.

Questions to ask in determining your framework might include:

- What behaviors do we see that clash with our values?
- How much energy can we realistically expend on attitude behaviors?
- What are we willing to tolerate?
- How will we reinforce the behavior we expect from our child?
- How will we manage attitude behaviors when we see them?
- Do these behaviors occur in different ways, depending on which one of us our child is dealing with at the moment?

That last question is a really interesting one, because kids respond differently to each parent. It can be incredibly stressful when one individual feels as if the other is a better or worse parent because of the results in the behavior of your child. One may say, "If you would do it my way, it'll

> *Two parents can say the same words and provoke different reactions.*

work!" But two parents can say the same words and take the same actions and yet provoke very different reactions from their child. There are many reasons for this, including the gender of a parent or a child, their history, temperament, tone of voice, delivery, and so forth. The bottom line is that the difference in response is a reality. And no matter which side you fall on, you have to parent from your own reality.

Understand the Intent Behind Behaviors

When you're dealing with attitude behaviors, you have to understand what's actually under your control and what's not. You can force a particular behavior, but you can't necessarily change the intent behind that behavior.

If you've ever tried to force your child to apologize to another for an insult, then you know that you can impel the apology as restitution, but it may be delivered in a snotty tone of voice. You can force your child to restate the apology without the tone, but you can't make her mean it. This can quickly devolve into a struggle of wills.

For instance, Sammi and her brother Micah were always bickering and often had to be corrected. She really pressed her father's buttons by adding her own snarky caveat to every apology she had to give her brother, such as: "*SorrrrEEE* for bumping your arm, but if you weren't so clumsy, you wouldn't have spilled the juice." Their dad was determined to correct this behavior, so every time Sammi did this, he would tell her to apologize more appropriately and force her to repeat it without the additional accusation. Was her father changing her intent? Absolutely not. Was he changing her behavior? Absolutely. It took a while, but eventually Sammi learned that snarky comments only get her into more trouble. Micah mimicked his sister's tone a few times, but he learned the same lesson even faster.

Another attitude behavior where intent comes into play is lying. There's a distinction to be made about lying that is nuanced, but important, and it all has to do with the ABCs. There are two kinds of lies: the *denial of responsibility*, which is almost a primal instinct, and the *manipulative lie*, where the child has underlying intentions behind the words.

Here's an example with the common situation of spilled juice:

Scenario One: Mom sees spilled juice on the floor and a half-empty cup on the table near her son. All evidence points to him having spilled the juice, but she still asks whether he did it. When backed into a corner like that, the natural reaction is to deny responsibility, because in his unsophisticated mind he's simply trying to avoid a negative consequence. Mom then punishes him twice—a Time-Out for the lie denying responsibility, and then restitution for the spill by having to clean it up. He's in a bad mood from the Time-Out, and gets really mad during cleanup, causing Mom to send him to Time-Out yet again for his attitude.

Antecedent. He spills his juice.

Behavior. He insists, "It wasn't me! I don't know how that juice got there."

Consequence. He's punished, but doesn't learn how to avoid spilling, or what he did wrong, by denying he made the spill. This doesn't make it any less likely the behavior will repeat, but more immediately it sets in motion a spiral of negative behavior and more consequences that are unnecessary.

One way for a parent to handle the denial of responsibility is to simply not ask the question of whether the child spilled the juice. The behavior his mom should be concerned with is her son being more careful carrying a cup. This means going straight to handling the spill, with a suggested consequence of the child doing cleanup. That is a natural lesson for the child: When something spills, you clean it up and be more careful next time.

Scenario Two: Mom sees spilled juice on the floor and a half-empty cup on the table near her son. When she looks at him, he points to his baby sister and lies, saying "She spilled my juice."

Antecedent. Same.

Behavior. He's now lying for a manipulative reason—to place the blame on his sister.

Consequence. This type of lying does need to be addressed, most appropriately with a negative consequence and an apology: "You can't blame your sister for this; she couldn't even have reached the juice cup to make it spill on the other side of the table. Get a paper towel to clean this up, and then you need to apologize to me and to her for lying. Since you're cleaning up, you go ahead and clean her highchair off, too. It's not nice to lie and try to get someone else in trouble."

Obviously, if there was really any doubt about who spilled the juice, Mom would have to handle this differently. But separating out the manipulative lie from the denial of responsibility helps avoid unnecessary stress and save energy for when she needs it more.

Use Strategies for Battling Attitude Behaviors

Adapting our Universal Strategies to address attitude behaviors by your child involves some nuance. Careful attention must be paid to the concept of reinforcement of behaviors, in terms of both reinforcing positive behaviors so that they are likely to be repeated and not reinforcing negative behaviors so that they are less likely to occur again.

Use Role-Modeling

The strategy of role-modeling lets your children know by example what kind of attitude behaviors you expect from them. They'll absorb those lessons covertly, but you'll see the results in the long run. Kids may not consciously idolize a parent, but they act the way those with whom they spend the most time act. If you don't want cussing, don't cuss. If you don't want eye rolling, don't roll your eyes. If you want attentiveness and responsiveness from your family, be attentive and responsive to them.

If you don't want eye rolling, don't roll your eyes.

There are occasions when you may see your child mimicking behaviors that your spouse or co-parent exhibits. It can be difficult to break a bad habit, and sometimes the individual isn't interested in changing his or her behavior. If you, your spouse, or co-parent can't stop, then you may decide that you'll be swimming upstream if you try to extinguish a behavior in your child that one of you continues to exhibit and that it's okay to let it go for now. Picking the battles you want to fight is central to reducing your stress.

One note on this idea of reinforcement for parents who are sarcastic themselves comes from Sara's personal experience: When we react with a response that's in the same timbre of sarcasm, the unintended effect is that the behavior in your child is modeled and reinforced and will happen more. Try hard to disengage and temper down your own natural response of sarcasm or smart-alecky comments and tone. If you find yourself using that tone, role-model your own correction: "Let me try that again." When your child gives you some attitude, she'll know just what you mean when you tell her to "try that again."

You should always be sure that your children understand that a particular behavior is not acceptable. Don't assume they know what presses your buttons. Tell them specifically which behaviors you don't like and won't accept.

Use Disengaging and Ignoring Attitude Behaviors

The strategies of disengaging and ignoring allow you to continue to function as a parent, and as a human being, despite attitudes emanating from your child. It's all a matter of reinforcing the behavior you want to see repeated and not reinforcing other behaviors. Questions to run through as you're considering whether to ignore or disengage from an attitude behavior include:

- Will my attention reinforce the behavior?
- Is it worth spending my parenting energy combatting this behavior?
- If I ignore this, will it hurt anything or anyone?

With many of these attitude behaviors, careful reactions that do not reinforce the behavior can be most effective. Ignoring is that reverse-psychology strategy: Not giving any attention to a behavior makes it less likely that the behavior is repeated. At the very least, ignoring a behavior avoids escalation and, when it comes to attitude, which is all about control, that's important. It's hard to ignore something, though. You really have to work at it, so this is where you need to make sure that expenditure of energy is worth it.

Disengaging is the strategy of giving a neutral, superficial response that doesn't feed into the heightened emotions of a difficult situation. When you disengage, you won't get drawn into the fray, nor will you inadvertently reinforce negative behavior. Give your child a direction and then turn your back and walk away. In that way, any additional sass falls on your "deaf" ears.

Manage Circumstances of Attitude Behavior

The strategy of managing the circumstances that contribute to attitude is an important one. Beyond your child having seen a parent, peer, or sibling role-model attitude, look at the circumstances around his or her behavior for clues as to why attitude is coming out at this particular moment. When your child is around friends, he may exhibit more attitude than in private for a variety of reasons (see the discussion of peer influence in Chapter 8). But there are plenty of other factors that can contribute to sassy replies or a negative attitude.

Stress can be a major precursor of attitude. A child who is stressed, whether it's the upcoming third-grade high-stakes standardized test or a sport/club competition, may manifest her fears through an attitude. She may project bravado as she tries to mask her fears or simply get annoyed at you for trying to help. Some children get so fussy at a parent during competitive events from dance recitals to soccer games that they don't even want their parent to watch. As difficult as it may be, try to look through the attitude to the emotions behind it.

Communicate Confidence in Your Child's Competence

When your child shows an attitude, he may be trying to assert some independence, and your reactions get translated into his brain in one of two ways: Either you think he can handle the task independently or you think he can't. Regardless of whether you

When your child shows an attitude, he may be trying to assert some independence.

really think either one of those things is irrelevant, it's what your child believes you are saying through your actions.

Consider the child who wants to tie her own shoes and strongly resists the parent's attempt to help, despite the fact that it is taking forever and she is now late leaving the house. She wants to do it herself to demonstrate competence. By intervening, the parent communicates a lack of confidence in the child's competence, and the child then reacts out of frustration, possibly to the tune of a tantrum.

How you interact with your children communicates your confidence in them. Sometimes attitude comes through if they're resisting us simply to prove *they can do it*. This is most clear in the example of physical separation attitudes: not wanting to hold your hand while walking across the street, or asking to get dropped off at the front of the school instead of being walked all the way inside. Your children are striving to be independent, and communicating that they can handle these kinds of tasks. All this may result in attitude behaviors as they express their resistance

> *How you interact with your children communicates your confidence in them.*

to your way of doing something. Of course, you have to make these kinds of physical separation decisions based on your children's safety, but respecting their feelings enough to at least find some ways to allow them more independence on a case-by-case basis can make a difference in their attitude. For example: "Okay, honey, I know you don't want to hold my hand crossing the street any more, but I'm worried about how fast the cars go on Main Street. So, let's make a deal. On Main Street, I'll hold onto your elbow, instead of holding your hand, and then on the smaller roads, you can walk across on your own. Deal?"

Choose When to Use Negative Consequences

Particularly when dealing with your child's more severe, repetitive attitude behaviors, there may come a point when the situation escalates and you decide that the strategies you've tried haven't been enough to stop the behavior. In assessing the situation, if you feel that you need to provide more of a deterrent, you might choose to institute some negative consequences.

Let's take a scenario involving foul language:

Scenario One: Eight-year-old Rashid hears his older cousin using swear words with his friends when their parents aren't around. He really looks up to and emulates his cousin, so it's not entirely surprising when he starts using some of the same words. When one day he calls his sister an offensive name, Rashid's parents tell him that such language is not allowed in their family.

They refuse to act shocked at the bad word, so that they don't give him any reinforcing attention for using it.

Antecedent: Rashid wants to be like his older cousin and starts mimicking swear words.

Behavior: Rashid calls his sister an offensive word.

Consequence: Rashid's parents educate Rashid but otherwise ignore the behavior, which they think is the right approach. In some cases it is, especially when a child is using the language to get a rise out of parents. If the child doesn't get any attention, he stops using that language. However, in this case, Rashid's cousin is providing plenty of reinforcement by making him feel cool. As a result, it's more likely the behavior will occur again.

Scenario Two: The same behavior occurs, but Rashid's parents are now clued in and ratchet up their reaction. They're ready with what they feel is a potent negative consequence—something their son will not like and will try to avoid in the future. They place a jar in the kitchen and institute a new rule: Any time anyone in the house swears, that person has to put a dollar in the "swear jar." Rashid has been saving up every penny to buy a new video game, so this hits him hard. He now tries hard *not* to swear.

Antecedent: Same.

Behavior: Same.

Consequence: Rashid's parents have hit on a great negative consequence: money. Their son values his savings and doesn't like giving any of it up. His behavior is now *less* likely to repeat.

Scenario Three: This time around, Rashid hasn't been saving for a video game and he only intermittently does the chores he's assigned, so he doesn't get much of an allowance. His parents know that if they institute the "swear jar," they'll have to actually *loan* him money to pay these fines. This obviously won't work. Instead, they reassess the situation, look for another negative consequence, and have him write a formal apology letter to his sister, as well as take away his bike for the weekend.

Antecedent: Same.

Behavior: Same.

Consequence: The "swear jar," once a deterring negative consequence, has lost its potency, so Rashid's parents adapted their strategy and came up with a new, more effective negative consequence of paying restitution by writing the letter, and also by the loss of his bike. Rashid's behavior is *less* likely to repeat.

The key to finding an effective negative consequence is to find something that is meaningful to your child and then use it as leverage.

• • •

Dealing with your child's attitude behaviors is one of those aspects of parenting that can run the gamut from downright annoying to bittersweet. You have to pick your battles carefully by looking at them through the lens of your family's value system. Your child's first foray into independence will mean behaviors that challenge your calm reactions at times, but by using the Universal Strategies of role-modeling and disengaging and ignoring, you'll be able to navigate these rocky waters while preserving your positive relationship with your child. As with many behaviors, managing the contributing factors is important, but so is remaining consistent and communicating confidence in your child's ability to handle something. In the big picture of discipline as education, you guide your children toward more appropriate ways to show independence, and the attitude behavior will dissipate. This will all pay off in dividends in a few years when you're looking for the light at the end of the tween-and-teen tunnel.

PART III

Develop Positive Characteristics

8

Impact Your Child's Social Development and Peer Influence

ou are the most important influence in your child's life. Your influence goes to the core of who your child is, and the person he or she is becoming. You may not see the full effects of your influence for a number of years, as friendships eventually take center stage, but, rest assured, it's critical.

A child's *social development*—the process of learning the knowledge, values, and skills that enable him to relate to peers and adults in a socially acceptable way—impacts his behavior.

You play a vital role in that development, first as the gatekeeper of your child's social relationships, then as the facilitator, and at times even as the arbitrator. There are numerous ways in which you can instill positive qualities in your child that spur social development.

> *You can instill positive qualities in your child that spur social development.*

When it comes to behavior, it's important to consider the impact of *peer influence*—the pressure on your child to conform to the actions and/or values of her peer group. This influence includes the reinforcing roles of her social group and the beginnings of peer pressure. From the friendships you facilitate in her early years through those she chooses in a school setting, the children your child hangs around with will influence her greatly.

Even *sibling rivalry*, the competition between children for their parents' attention, can have an influence on their social development. Setting a solid social foundation can help your kids feel happier, more connected, and less vulnerable to those negative influences they will encounter in the years to come. While you can have a huge impact on their social development, it's important to act early, because your influence will be nudged out temporarily during adolescence and replaced by peer influence.

In this chapter, we discuss the positive aspects of your child's development of social skills in relating to other children, and examine the role of peer influence. (We've heavily covered the aspect of your child's social development with you in the sections dealing with the Universal Strategy of cultivating a positive parent–child relationship.) We connect the dots between peer-pressure behaviors in adolescence and healthy peer-group choices in the 3-to-11-year-old age range. From the origins of sibling rivalry behavior to the steps you can take if your child has a hard time fitting into a peer group, there are many ways in which you can shape your child's behavior for positive social interactions.

Promote Positive Social Relationships with Peers

Don't underestimate the impact that relationships with peers have on your child's social development. Having friendships is a *need*, not just a want, and it's *essential* for healthy development. This doesn't mean that every child has to have a huge social network or be a social butterfly; it's okay for an introverted child to have fewer friends than an extrovert.

Kids need to be fulfilled by having some social relationships with friends.

The point is that kids need to be fulfilled by having some social relationships with friends.

It's well established in psychological research that preschool-aged children who have positive peer relationships are likely to maintain these positive interactions in grade school. On the other hand, children who don't have the skills to play constructively and develop friendships with other children their age can be excluded later on and lose the opportunity to develop additional and more complex social skills that are essential for future peer interaction.

Positive social development comes partly from innate social competence—some of us are more naturally "social" than others—and partly from social practice. With exposure to more opportunities to try different social behaviors, your child will be able to hone and refine his skills through natural feedback from those with whom he's interacting.

There are some very easy, proactive ways you can enhance your child's social skills and help him make the most of his social opportunities using our Universal Strategies.

First, give your child many chances to play with other children and to negotiate, share, and deal with problems that arise. Join a playgroup, find kids on the block, or connect through your faith-based organization. This is the Universal Strategy of practice sessions, built right into the neighborhood playground. Pair it with the coaching strategy and use plenty of praise for the

Your Child's Set of Social Skills

Taking stock of your child's social skills today can help you determine where you may need to offer assistance or reinforcement. Some of us are just better at social interactions than others. Use this activity to reflect on your child's ability to:

Social Ability	No Skills	Some Skills	Good Skills
Make friends			
Retain friends			
Play one-on-one			
Play as a group or team member			
Pick up on social cues			
Change activities			
Lead activities			
Deal with conflict			
Join a group where he or she doesn't know anyone			
Handle teasing			
Other: _____			

Seeing it laid out in this manner should give you some clues as to where your involvement can assist your child. No one is going to be perfect at all of these skills, but *all* of them are skills you and your child can work to improve.

behaviors you see that you like. Don't try to control every inter-action; let minor squabbles play out a little before deciding to get involved. These natural oppor-tunities for conflict resolution are invaluable in helping kids develop social skills.

Natural opportunities for conflict resolution are invaluable in helping kids develop social skills.

Second, use the Universal Strategy of cultivating a positive relationship and take some time to play with your child as a peer would play. Children are able to learn a great deal through play with a parent, even though it can be difficult to drop the "parent" persona. Your child's social competence will be enhanced every time you laugh and every time you're responsive to her ideas on what to play.

Resist the urge to direct these play periods. Let your child take the lead while you're in the supporting role of playmate. Do offer constructive feedback, however. When she has trouble waiting her turn, let her know that other kids might not like that and may not want to keep playing with her as a result. As they get older, you can continue with playtime on the basketball court or with board games, either of which provide the perfect setup for practicing important social skills, such as turn-taking, dealing with disputes, and winning or losing with grace.

Third, whether watching your own child or people watch-ing at a public place, use the Universal Strategy of positive re-inforcement and name the social behaviors that you want your child to repeat or emulate. It's very important to specifically comment on those behaviors and attributes that you want to reinforce in your child's social development. Here are a few examples:

- "I saw you share your new doll with Cassidy today. I know your doll's special, and you probably were worried she might get dirty or her hair might get messed up, but you could see how much Cassidy wanted to play with her. That was very nice. And you know what? Cassidy was really careful, wasn't she? She really knows how to take care of her friends' toys."

- "Wow, do you see that little boy just coming off of the field? His team lost, but he smiled as he was shaking hands with the other team's players and kept telling them it was a great game. Some of his teammates seemed like they were pouting, but he had a great attitude."

- "You know, Benjamin's mom called me today to ask if you were still mad at him. I guess you guys got upset with each other the other day when you were at his house? She told me Benjamin was yelling but you kept calm, and I was glad to hear that you behaved yourself even though you were mad. So what happened?"

Manage Access to Peer Influencers

While you can't choose your child's friends, you certainly can control access to those peers with whom your child plays. Especially when kids are younger, you can choose your child's playdates and decide whether to accept invitations. Kids should always be exposed to a great diversity of peers, but it's okay to steer clear of one whom you feel is objectionable, like the aggressive kid in the playgroup or the foul-mouthed one at daycare.

It's important to play a central role early on in facilitating social development for your child. Numerous factors, including parent role-modeling and early friendships, give children a basis for selecting the characteristics they like in others. So being thoughtful now means you have the opportunity to impact the types of characteristics your child will find desirable in friends later on.

As your child gets older, you necessarily must relinquish some of the control and trust that your positive influence will hold, even when your child is away from you, because of the foundation you've built of open and honest communication, appropriate limit setting, and modeling of good social values and characteristics. Within this environment, the negative influence of a peer is much more likely to be seen as undesirable by your child, and the relationship is more likely to be short lived.

But the occasional bad influence from a peer is inevitable. When this happens, try to understand the underlying reason. For example, your child may need a boost of self-confidence in order to stand up to the negative influence, or she may be worried that if she stands up to this kid, she may not find another friend. It may be that she's just attracted to the short-term excitement or rebelliousness this child offers, or she may not know the right words to tell this child to stop. It could be even as simple as the fact that this child lives nearby and is always available to play at the same time as your child.

> *The occasional bad influence from a peer is inevitable.*

Regardless of the reason for this friendship, it's important not to criticize your child's choice of friends. Often, children will become defensive and may continue to interact with these friends out of a sense of loyalty or to rebel against parents. Instead, focus on the specific behaviors you observe and be certain your child understands that there will be consequences for any negative behaviors.

For example, if your child engages in a bad behavior when he's with a friend, a natural consequence of this would be to restrict access to that friend temporarily. If the bad behavior resulted in damages to property or someone's feelings, you can use the Universal Strategy of having your child make apologies and restitution (and if you can swing it with the other child's parents, the friend should do the same). Additionally, you can use the Universal Strategy of negative consequences in the form of restricting privileges.

It's also important that your child see your willingness to discipline his friend when they're at your home. It's appropriate for a parent to set clear house rules for any visitors, as well as to have clear consequences for breaking those house rules: "It is not okay that you guys were throwing your sister's Teddy bear into the garbage can, so you two need to say 'sorry' and then clean the bear off."

Later on, you can use an *if/then* statement from the Universal Strategy of giving good directions and say privately to your child, "I notice that you tend to misbehave more when you hang out with Michael. Every family has different rules, and I don't know what his are, but I need for you to remember *our* rules and let your friends know what they are when they're here. *If* you can behave responsibly when Michael's here, *then* we can keep setting up playdates with him."

Combat Negative Peer-Group Behaviors

Peer pressure can be both positive and negative.

We're all subject to peer pressure—the drive we feel either directly or indirectly to conform to the norm set by our social group. Adopting characteristics of those around us can give us a sense of belonging and acceptance. Peer pressure can be both positive and negative. But as we said in the beginning of this chapter, children who have a solid social foundation and a generally positive peer network are less likely to be influenced by negative peers.

To use an example well trod in the media about peer pressure leading to drug usage in teens, it's true that some children can be taken in by that kind of negative peer pressure. But, as we learned in physics, for every action there is an equal and opposite reaction. An example of *positive* peer pressure is the high achiever whose peer group consists of other high achievers, and who as a result is more likely to shun the drug culture at school because it's inconsistent with his peer group.

In children ages 3 to 11, you're more likely to see tagalong behavior or group behavior. Typically, something looks like fun, a bunch of kids are doing it, and your kid wants to do it, too.

Positive group behavior can spur achievement, attention to manners, and healthy choices. But it's when a group reinforces negative behavior that our blood pressure rises. One of the best ways to help your child resist negative peer pressure is by helping her develop a positive self-esteem and a positive sense of self-worth. This can help her stand up in the face of negative peer pressure so she won't be so vulnerable to the need to fit in. In other words, a happy child whose social and emotional needs are met and one who thinks well of herself is much less likely to feel the need to give in to negative peer pressure.

Teach your child to be assertive. Children who are afraid to stand up for themselves tend to have difficulty handling stressful

A child whose social and emotional needs are met is less likely to give in to peer pressure.

situations. Use the Universal Strategy of practice sessions to teach specific "turn-down" comments. By developing and practicing possible scenarios, you can help him come up with ways to say *no.* These allow him to stand up for himself in an appropriate, nonaggressive manner.

Here are some age-appropriate examples of topics for turn-down comments you can use with your child to combat negative group behavior:

- "Has anyone you know ever looked at your answers on a test and tried to copy them? That happened to me a few times when I was your age. Cheating isn't right, and it's against the school rules. If that ever does happen to you, just tell the other kid to stop and if he or she doesn't, let the teacher know."
- "I heard a story the other day about kids your age, but they were from another state. The story was about how much trouble they all got in for lying. They told a bunch of lies and it kept causing more and more problems. We *always* tell the truth in our family, and you can say that to anyone who ever asks you to lie, okay?"

It's important to realize that as your child develops, the negative pressures will change. Therefore, practice of these turn-down comments must be ongoing and topical rather than a one-time thing. Eventually, you'll start using more serious scenarios to practice, like drugs, alcohol, and other risky behaviors. Keep the practice sessions short and to the point, and only offer them up on a sporadic basis so your child doesn't tune you out. If he's used to the idea that it's okay to say *no* from earlier situations, he'll be more empowered to do so when he's a teen and the ramifications of his choices are much greater.

Use Strategies When Your Child Has Peer-Group Problems

Some children experience trouble fitting in with a peer group for a variety of reasons. In some cases, a dynamic changes in a group and members drift off, leaving your child left out. In other cases, your child may just not be as naturally gifted in social circles and struggles to fit in. Occasionally, a child is targeted for ostracism and bullying.

It's important to take action to help your child with peer-group problems because children who have trouble fitting into social groups are more likely to be vulnerable to negative peer pressure. From a child's perspective, it often feels more comfortable to fit in with *any* group, even a negative one, as opposed to not

> *It feels more comfortable to fit in with* any *group, as opposed to not fitting in at all.*

fitting in at all. Remember that friendships are a *need*, essential to just about every individual. So when a child gravitates toward playmates who tend to be aggressive or manipulative, or who otherwise exhibit social behaviors that we don't agree with, it's often the case that the child is having trouble getting her social needs met in a more positive way.

A child who reaches adolescence and is not having his or her social needs met by socially competent and secure peers but is instead hanging out with others on the social fringe may be more willing to engage in negative behaviors, negative relationships, and risk-taking behaviors in order to gain social acceptance. While this can be a little ways off from the 3-to-11-year-old age range of this book, the seeds of positive social development are sown in these early years.

If your child is having peer-group problems, regardless of whether this is a temporary or chronic situation, there are some steps you can take to help your child improve socialization skills and foster the identification and growth of potential positive friendships:

- Play to his strengths by signing him up for lessons, a team, or a club where there will be access to other children with similar interests.
- Host regular movie nights or pizza parties for the whole team or club in which your child is involved. Make sure it's something that will be enticing enough for these acquaintances to want to attend. This provides the opportunity for you to observe your child's social behavior and provide feedback. Additionally, an acquaintance has more of a possibility of turning into a friend in this kind of a fun social setting.
- If your child gets along and is more comfortable with other children who are a couple of years younger but doesn't seem to connect well with kids her age, then facilitate playtime with those younger ones so that she gets as much social practice time in as possible. Allowing her to stay within her comfort zone helps her learn more in a safe space than if you pushed her to only associate with peers her own age.
- Consult your child's teacher or school guidance counselor to get some context as to what's going on. A teacher may be able to identify a child with whom your child is friendly in class and you can then help cultivate that relationship.
- Seek out a social skills group for your child. This is a relatively new type of support group, specifically intended to generate

positive social interactions, that is becoming increasingly common in cities and towns across the United States.

Throughout these action steps, you'll need to use the coaching and praising Universal Strategies liberally. Have a discussion with your child just before he enters the club meeting or team practice or right before all the kids from those groups come over for pizza. Be *very specific* in terms of naming the behavioral tendencies you want him to show. You can even practice what he'll say to the other kids with simple interactions like basic greetings and asking to join in play.

For example, if your child tends to be very blunt with other kids, thereby turning them off, you need to be proactive and say exactly that: "When your teammates arrive, you need to remember how to be polite. Think about your words carefully, and how the other person will feel when you say them. I heard you tell Xavier that his clothes didn't match last week, and that hurt his feelings. While you may have been right, it really shouldn't matter to you what he wears, so just don't say things like that. Instead, you can offer everyone something to drink and show them your playroom. Do you understand?"

You're soliciting your child's agreement that he'll work to manage his social behavior, and you've given him a specific example. Prompt him again just as he's entering, and even *during*, the event once or twice if necessary. The idea is that he'll then be more likely to self-manage that behavior.

In the event that your child becomes an active target or other children are seeking out your child for repeated negative interactions, immediately speak with your child's school principal, team coach, or club director. Bullying and rejection can cut a child like a knife and have lasting effects. School and extracur-

Bullying and rejection can cut a child like a knife.

ricular activities should be safe places, but if your child is a target, he is anything but safe. Find out how long the behavior has been going on; this will help you make a determination as to whether to speak with a counselor or mental health professional. Chapter 11 has additional information on how to know when you need to seek professional input.

Handle Sibling Rivalry

As children develop, they use the social group of their family and their siblings as a natural test market for the wider world of social behavior. While it's not exactly the same as with peers due to the circumstances of living together, from sharing to turn-taking to conflict resolution, you have a natural setup for observing, reinforcing, practicing, and coaching social behaviors in your kids. Of course, sibling rivalry often rears its ugly head, and this can cause us to lose sight of the social aspects of sibling interaction. Regardless, it's important to recognize all the opportunities you have to encourage social behavior by focusing on sibling interactions, even in the face of jealousy and rivalry.

Like many of the behaviors we've discussed in this book, sibling rivalry is completely natural. In the science of biology, when you have more than one organism vying for finite resources of basic needs, there's a natural competition that develops. This is akin to the hypothesis of "survival of the fittest." Those organisms that can get the most resources survive. In a family with more than one child, these basic instincts for survival come to the surface in sibling rivalry. Today, in our society, two or more children aren't vying for actual *survival*, but they are competing for the limited resources of a parent: time and attention.

Additionally, you have contributing factors such as the dynamics of individual relationships between each member of the family, and the individual characteristics of each person, with which

> *Siblings are competing for the limited resources of a parent: time and attention.*

to contend. You can do everything right as a parent and still never be able to eliminate sibling rivalry, but that shouldn't necessarily be your goal. Maintaining civility, so you don't have kids who are at each other's throats all the time, is a fine goal when you have protracted sibling rivalry. Often, in time the rivalry fades and the relationship between siblings grows into one of tolerance and sometimes actual friendship when they're older. You do want them to be able to get along when they're grownups, but you can't make a kid like his brother or sister. Civility toward one another is important and can be expected, enforced, and reinforced.

Many aspects of civil behavior between siblings revolve around attitude. All of the ways to use our Universal Strategies explained in Chapter 7 for attitude behaviors can also apply to sibling rivalry behaviors. Remember that you need to pick your battles wisely, determine those behaviors you'll prioritize as requiring action, and apply them equitably to both, or all, of your children. Always keep in mind that sometimes the wisest course is to let a conflict play out to see whether your kids can work it out on their own. If they can, it's time for lots of praise that calls attention to how they reached this achievement.

> *Sometimes the wisest course is to see whether your kids can work it out on their own.*

Sibling rivalry offers a perfect use of the Universal Strategy of redirecting focus by changing the attention from the problem to finding ways to get along. Redirecting your children's focus negates the myriad of triggers that siblings use to get into it with each other. When you sense that they're headed down the path of competition or jealousy or frustration with each other, assign them a task, invite them to start a new game, or separate them.

Some parents insist on implementing consequences to both siblings involved, to underscore the idea that it takes them both (or all) to work together to get along. That's a subjective decision best made by you based on either your priorities or what's going on at that moment. We advocate for equitable parenting, which is being fair but adapting your strategies to each child as necessary.

Rivalry aside, however, some aspects of peer influences can be mimicked by siblings. Group dynamics begin in the earliest years, and the first group your child is a part of is your family. Our Universal Strategy of cultivating a positive relationship with your child can play a *huge* role in dealing with both sibling and peer influence. Like many concepts in parenting, this one has many layers, but the foundation is self-esteem, self-worth, and a sense of belonging. When we parent each of our children from the very beginning equitably and with respect, positive communication, nurturance, and clear boundaries, we help foster that solid foundation.

• • •

From sibling rivalry to peer-influence groups to outright peer pressure, the social development of your children is yet another place where behavior plays an important part, and you can use specific strategies to shape positive behavior. Understanding the need of children to have interactions and close ties to a social group will help you build on the foundation of social development you've already established within your own family. That very foundation will be what your children rely on when they're facing peer pressure and choosing friends, and while they may make mistakes from time to time, they'll come back to their parents, their core influencers, for guidance and support when needed. You're the most important people in their lives whether they admit it or not.

9

Instill Resilience and Grit in Your Child

One of the most enduring and valuable sets of skills that we can instill in our children is a sense of resilience in the face of stress or perceived failure. Sometimes termed *grit*, this "pull yourself up from your bootstraps" mentality is characterized by tenacity, problem solving, and the ability to continue to strive for success despite setbacks. The process of problem solving has leapfrogged innate intelligence and learned skills to be a highly prized quality in an individual.

Resilience partly stems from a person's temperament, but it's also a skill that can be learned and practiced throughout childhood in order for it to be well developed in adulthood. *Resilience* is that ability to adapt to challenges and setbacks and keep on trying, while the term *grit* adds the implication of strength and fortitude in the face of problems—the confidence to try to overcome instead of feeling like a victim of circumstance. Grit and resilience affect a child's behavior in many positive ways.

In this chapter, you'll learn how resilience and grit can be nurtured by having confidence and using praise. You'll see how mistakes like locking your keys in your car gives you a great opportunity to be a role model. Reserves of resilience can even help stress-proof your child. But the first step toward grittiness is allowing your child the opportunity to learn from failure.

Let Your Child Experience Failure

Adults sometimes handle rejection or failure as a temporary setback that's simply an obstacle to be overcome. Others are virtually debilitated by them to the point of avoiding taking any kinds of risks whatsoever. It is the same with children; however, when kids learn resilience during their formative years, they are well equipped to skillfully manage life's ups and downs as adults. Without taking a risk there's never a chance of beating the odds and succeeding at your wildest goal. Without failure there can never be a successful comeback.

> *When kids learn resilience, they are well equipped to manage life's ups and downs.*

Remember what we explained in the beginning of this book: Discipline is a form of education, of shaping your child's behavior in positive directions. A child who learns from her mistakes will be able to deal with adversity in an adaptive way. These adaptations mean she'll be able to start shaping her own behavior. That ability to adapt is a big part of resilience and grit, because she's learning how to solve or work around a problem in a constructive way that clears the path to success.

Letting your child experience failure or disappointment is the first step to building a healthy sense of resilience. Too often, parents work on making sure their kids feel good about themselves as opposed to making sure they can cope with life's bumps and bruises. We can find it hard to loosen our protective instincts and allow our children to get into situations where they may not succeed, much less ones where the chances for success are nil. We want to swoop in and alleviate their pain.

Swooping Situations

Think about the last time you swooped in and either rescued your child from a potentially difficult situation or took over for him on a frustrating task. What was going on at that moment?

_____

_____

_____

Now, think about what your child could have learned from the situation if you hadn't jumped in.

_____

_____

_____

Take this information and, the next time this situation or a similar one presents itself, remember how problem solving on his own can add to your child's resilience. Take a step back, and watch how your child tries to figure out a solution. If asked, you can offer a bit of advice, and then inquire, "What do *you* think?"

By being overly protective, we rob our children of the growth potential that comes from picking themselves back up after failure, brushing off the dust, and redoubling their efforts toward their goal. The benefits are cyclical: These efforts bolster their sense of self-confidence and self-reliance, which in turn reinforces the way they bounce back from the next failure.

> *Childhood is filled with natural opportunities to learn to cope effectively with failure.*

Letting your child fail doesn't mean putting her into a situation where failure is certain. Nor does it mean exposing your child to undue stress or pressure. Childhood is filled with natural opportunities for children to learn to cope effectively with stress, pressure, possible rejection, and failure. Being open to the possibility of failure and not letting it scare you, or them, is what gives them those important learning opportunities. Here are a few tips:

- *Don't always let them win at board games.* When they're very little and first learning, let them get excited about winning a game against you. You don't have to be a cutthroat property developer in *Monopoly* or attempt manifest destiny in *Risk*, but once your kids understand the game, play them for real. You can use the coaching strategy to talk with them before the game about how they'll feel if they don't win.
- *Resist the urge to take over school projects.* So his handwriting is crooked, and he didn't color inside the lines. The child who completes a school project on his own is infinitely more confident of his skills than the one who gets an A by turning in something done by a parent. (Teachers *can* tell the difference.) As stated in Chapter 4, you want to instill a motivation for learning.
- *In sports, don't skip a competition against the unbeatable team; send your kid right on out to that field to play her heart out.* After the loss, don't complain that the other kids were so much bigger or that the referees made biased calls. Instead, use the praise

strategy to compliment your child's hustle, the way she dog-
gedly went after the ball time and time again, or the way she
rallied her team to keep trying until the bitter end. Then, savor
the opportunity to bond by commiserating the loss over a
well-deserved ice cream.

Grit Doesn't Mean Being as Tough as Nails

While developing grit includes strength, fortitude, and establishing a protectively thick skin for criticism, setbacks, and failure,
it doesn't mean that you're trying to make your kid as tough as
nails. The word *grit* sometimes connotes an image like Clint East-
wood in those old Spaghetti Westerns: dusty cowboy hat, eyes
squinting against the harsh sun, cigar clenched between his
teeth—a tough guy who can handle anything and doesn't need
anyone to help him.

Children can become tough, but should not be expected to become hardened.

That is *not* what we mean by
grit. Children can become tough,
but should not be expected to
become hardened to failure or
setbacks; rather, we want them
to *learn from those experiences.* But
make no mistake about it: These
can be very hard, sometimes heart-
breaking lessons for your children.
Helping them through does not mean taking a tough-as-nails approach with them, just as it doesn't mean you coddle them and
make excuses for a failure. Fostering resilience means striking a
balance between being empathetic, determined, supportive, and
a role model for how to handle themselves.

When your child has experienced a rejection or failure isn't
the time to be overly critical. Try to view the situation through

his eyes so you can understand and validate his feelings. This does two things: It gives him the words to express these feelings and leads him to be more receptive later on when you can discuss problem solving for future situations. If he failed, you're not simply saying that was okay; you're communicating with him about the emotions he's feeling. Don't expect him to brush off a loss immediately; expect him to be sad and mad, and name those feelings for him. When he's past these emotions, perhaps later that day or the next day you can have a conversation about using those feelings to do things differently next time.

Have Confidence and Use Praise

We wrote about communicating confidence in your child's competence in Chapter 8, and that certainly comes into play when developing resilience. Communicating confidence stems from attentive, active parenting, which allows for spontaneous, positive engagement, conveys sureness of a child's ability to handle herself, and ensures an openness so the child can ask for help when needed. Let us be very clear: We are not advocating that you hover, smother, and engage in every minute aspect of your child's life like a helicopter. That's not being attentive, and actually will sap a child's ability to develop resilience.

Here's the difference between being a helicopter parent and being an attentive parent:

- *Helicopter Parenting.* You help your child with her science fair project by planning out the presentation and the project display, lining up each photo for her (so they're perfectly even), and using your calligraphy skills for the header. Any time there's a direction she doesn't understand, you email or call the teacher instead of letting your child get clarification in class. You supervise the way she uses inflection in her voice during the presentation, and then stand on the side of the auditorium mouthing the words, ready to cue her with the next line if necessary. After the presentation is complete, you tell your child how great a job "we" did and then collapse from exhaustion that evening.

- *Attentive Parenting.* You talk with your child about her science project, complimenting her on choosing an interesting subject, and getting her the supplies she tells you she needs. When she asks for help lining up the photos correctly, you hand her a ruler to show her how. You also help her search online for calligraphy templates. Your child gets clarifications on the directions from her teacher and says she doesn't want to practice her presentation in front of you because she wants to surprise you. In the auditorium, you proudly videotape her presentation from your seat in the third row and later take her out for some ice cream to celebrate her accomplishment.

When you hover like a helicopter, you're transmitting the idea that you don't believe your child is able to do something on her own. That's not the message you want your kids to hear or feel. In order to build up her resilience, have faith in her strengths, make sure she knows it, and let go of your parental instinct to do it for her.

Support your children to try, succeed, or fail, and then, to try again.

We all know that our kids aren't good at *everything*. No one is. While you want to communicate confidence in your children, it's important to help them keep it all in perspective. Support your children to try, to succeed or to fail, and then, if they so choose, to try again. It's important that children take the lead on resilience when possible. Try not to interfere in your children's process of bouncing back before they have a chance to cope independently. We recognize our children's strengths and weaknesses and love them unconditionally. Keep your own goals for them realistic, so you're not pushing them hard in a direction in which they have no interest in going, but guiding them to set realistic and achievable goals for themselves.

Little League can be a great microcosm of this concept. Your son wants to play, so you sign him up, get him a glove, and start playing catch in the backyard. (As much as you're tempted to picture him in the uniform of your favorite team someday, you keep your expectations reasonable.) The season starts and the coach doesn't put him in the batting lineup. Your son is upset because he feels like all the other kids are better than he is, and he tells you he wants to quit. Having paid to join, you let him know he needs to at least finish out the season.

You talk with him about how all the great players have to practice every day to be great and offer to help him improve his hitting by taking him to the batting cages. He consents, and you start him off with very slow pitches and eventually increase to game speed. Your son improves his hitting skills, and you point out the link between his work and his success to him: "Your hard work is paying off; when you first started at the cages, you only hit two out of every five pitches, but now you're hitting three or four pitches. Way to go!"

Does the coach put him in the batting lineup after this? Maybe; maybe not. Have you increased his grit and aptitude? Absolutely. Your son may sense his improvement and really love the game enough to play again next season, or decide to try another activity instead. Either way, he understands that when things don't go the way he wants them to, there are things he

Reinforce your children's efforts, not simply their ability.

can do to make them better. He's started to develop a resilience and work ethic that will benefit his future endeavors.

Praising your children's contributions to their own success is also important, but a nuanced concept. You want to reinforce your children's efforts, not simply their ability. Be careful not to praise any child for natural talents—innate intelligence, athletic ability or musical aptitude—that come without effort. Kids who are blessed with natural talents are certainly fortunate, but the child didn't "do" anything to get that natural talent. Hard work, perseverance, and a willingness to take risks and cope with mistakes is what your child does have control over. So instead of saying something like, "Wow, you are so smart," to a bright child who does well at the school spelling bee, consider using a different kind of praise, such as, "Wow, you've worked so hard and studied all those words every day for a week, and see how that pays off? Well done!"

Problem-Solve Like a Role Model

As with nearly every behavioral issue that arises with your children, being a role model will help you in shaping their behavior in a positive way. When it comes to resilience and grit, modeling good problem-solving skills will have exponential effects.

Consider these situations, and think about your own reaction to them:

- Locking your keys in the car
- Forgetting something important at home

- Putting together furniture or birthday presents with lots of pieces
- Having to fix the TV settings that have gotten messed up
- Mixing up your days and forgetting your child has practice
- Checking luggage for a flight and finding your bag is over the size limit

Are you laughing, thinking about your reactions to all these situations? These are the moments during which you're building your child's sense of problem-solving skills. The most effective learning happens from watching you, so role-model thoughtfulness, ingenuity, patience, reading directions, stick-to-itiveness, and asking for help when it's needed.

If you overreact to your own mistakes and setbacks, your child is more likely to fear making mistakes and start to avoid risks. This can lead to a child who seems to be a perfectionist and falls apart in the face of even minor setbacks.

Store Up Reserves of Resilience for Challenging Times

Like a savings account at a bank in which you deposit a portion of your paycheck every month, building up a reserve of funds on which you can draw when an unexpected problem pops up, when you're teaching your child to have grit you're banking reserves of grit for them to pull out when a setback occurs.

These banked reserves can have protective properties, insulating and in effect stress-proofing your child. They allow her to endure more, cope better, or try something for the umpteenth time. The times that you have role-modeled patience contribute to these reserves, as does all the praise you've given for her hard

> *Each time she's failed, but got back up again, she has hit the jackpot of grit.*

work. Each time she's failed, but got back up again and finally succeeded, she has hit the jackpot of grit, filling up her reserves to overflowing.

Other contributors might include a solid social network of friends, family, and caring adults in her corner. Activities that make your child feel good about herself, such as volunteering or getting the opportunity to be a leader, also deposit into that same account. When stressors come about, your child is more likely to handle them easier, and with less disruption, than a child who doesn't have as much resilience in reserve.

But the reverse is also true. Any condition that create a sense of incompetence, such as social or learning problems, can be detrimental to resilience. There are plenty of opportunities growing up for a child to feel bad about herself. That's why building up those reserves of grit in every area of life you can is crucial, so that during those times when your child doesn't feel so confident, she can dig deep down and remember how much she has going for her in another area of life and draw on that reserved grit to bolster her in this situation.

• • •

Grit is good. Grit is powerful. Grit can endure throughout your child's life. It is, perhaps, the single most important quality you can nurture in your children, because, secondary to your love and discipline, grit can be a foundation to their overall wellbeing.

When you can, let your child have the opportunity to fail. Make sure she also has the chance to make a comeback after a failure. Work hard to avoid being overprotective, and make sure to communicate your confidence in her abilities. It's a constant balancing act between providing the right degree of challenge, the right number of opportunities to cope with failure, and a constant amount of unconditional love and acceptance.

Be the problem-solver that you want your children to be by showing them your own grit and resilience in the face of a challenge. And make deposits into their banked reserves every chance you get, which will form a protective, stress-proof shield around them. You'll see behavioral improvements as your children gain resilience, and you'll be preparing them to handle those bumps in the road that are sure to come at some point in the future. Above all, you'll be preparing your children for a future of success of their own making.

PART IV

Recognize Red Flags

10

Manage Situations That Increase Family Stress

*A*t different times in our lives, circumstances conspire to put more stress on us and our families. During these times, our coping mechanisms, and consequently our parenting skills, may need a boost—or a break. It's only natural: The human mind and body can take only so much stress before maximum capacity is reached, at which point we start to shut down or collapse.

Let's return to the metaphor with which we opened the book—that of a garden, where you've tilled the soil, planted the seeds, added fertilizer, and watered regularly. But now, just when you think your garden is taking shape, *bam!* Along comes a big storm that damages or, in some cases, devastates it. When you come up for air, you look around and see that your carefully planted rows are in disarray; plants have been pulled up completely, their roots exposed; and other plants have been crushed by the wind and rain.

When a serious situation rolls in like a storm hitting a garden, your family may feel similarly. A separation or divorce, the necessity for long-distance parenting, a grave illness or death, or even a financial issue like a home foreclosure can make you and your family feel as if you've been caught up in a tornado. In the aftermath, severe stress can occur. To children, even life events like a move or a new baby can make them feel as if their world has been turned upside down. A divorce can make a child feel as if his roots have been forcefully pulled out of the ground. An illness may crush your child's spirit. Feelings such as these can befall any family member, regardless of age, during and after a calamity.

In this chapter, we take you through a number of these kinds of situations that increase your family's stress and offer some tips on ways you can help either ease the burden from your children's shoulders or maintain some semblance of normalcy that allows them to feel secure while dealing with it. This chapter also underscores the need for you to take care of yourself; it may seem selfish, but it's really an investment in your child. To begin, you need to know what stress can look like and the behaviors you might see in your child that would indicate he or she is having trouble handling a situation.

Recognize the Symptoms of Stress

In a sense, stress is a state of mind for children and adults alike because it stems from an individual's unique perspective. Two people experiencing the same situation may cope differently; one may feel intense mental or emotional tension while the other experiences a slight bump in the road.

The very fact that a situation is unfamiliar or new, even if it's positive, can create anxiety and stress in your child. Sometimes this stems from an uncertainty as to what's going to happen. The reasons for your child's anxiety may feel irrational to you, but only when you find out what's going through her mind can you help her cope with the situation more capably.

If you've ever had an outgoing child who was suddenly reluctant to participate in a birthday party, you may have seen this firsthand. Typically, your child might have run straight over to check out the presents and the cake, but that time he hung at the door, holding onto your leg in a manner you thought had disappeared when he was younger. Perhaps the group was larger than usual, or the home at which the party took place was unfamiliar to him, so while you may have been surprised at his reaction, it was easier to figure out what was worrying him.

You may have experienced a more serious situation if you've ever gone through a divorce. Perhaps your daughter began to worry about whether Daddy would be going away forever because her best friend never saw her dad after her parents' divorce. It might have seemed illogical, because you had a schedule of visitation and co-parenting all worked out and had even explained it to her, but until she truly understood how it would work for *your* family, she was going to be really stressed.

Recognizing the symptoms of stress and then identifying the stressor is extremely important. Remember that children often express emotion through their behavior. A *change in behavior* is most often a key indicator of stress, and it should cause you to examine what's going on with your child to create this change.

If you notice changes in your child's typical behavior patterns along the lines of the following common symptoms, he or she may be experiencing stress. Any

A change in behavior is most often a key indicator of stress.

of these symptoms can occur during any type of stressful situation; there's not necessarily any rhyme or reason as to how children physically react to a stressor:

- Recurring physical discomfort, such as a tummy-ache on a school morning or a body-ache every day before practice, without presence of a health reason
- Avoidance behaviors, like saying they don't want to participate in something that they used to do frequently
- Emotional changes, such as an outgoing kid withdrawing, a normally happy child seeming sad all the time, or a mild-mannered child becoming irritable or developing an explosive temper
- School performance changes, such as plummeting grades or acting out in class
- Increased fears or anxiety
- Sleep changes, either trouble sleeping or sleeping much more than usual

It's critical to remain vigilant to unfolding and developing stresses. If your family is going, or has recently gone, through something that you know is difficult, such as any of the situations we present later in this chapter, these behaviors should be a red flag for you.

Your children may seem to have got over it in the short term, but for the big stressors it's not unusual for there to be residual effects and stress that reemerges. For some kids, that can occur over weeks, months, or even years. Sometimes, it may come back up at various developmental stages later in life, and the stress is reexperienced. Continuing to be open to questions and really listening to your children when they share their thoughts is imperative. Stressful situations are not a one-time conversation. And sometimes, there's one simple detail about a stressor that is affecting your child more than you might have thought and it's only when you listen to her concerns that you realize what that is.

In addition to caring attentively for your child during a troubled period, it's also important to be cognizant of the feelings you're experiencing. You—and any adult parenting your child—need to take care of yourself on a regular basis. When a stressful situation occurs, this is especially crucial. While it may seem selfish to focus on your own needs, this can make you more resistant to the negative effects of chronic stress. It's really an investment in your child, because taking care of yourself will make

Taking care of yourself will make you a more effective parent.

you a more effective parent. This includes making sure you are eating properly, exercising regularly, getting plenty of rest, taking some time for yourself, and having an emotional outlet.

If you're feeling emotionally overwhelmed, we urge you to seek out support. This becomes *critically necessary* if you're involved in the situation that is stressful, such as becoming ill or going through a divorce. During these times, you'll have your hands full with your own stress and reactions to the situation, and it's a monumental task to be a healthy parent as well. If you don't have a trusted friend or family member in whom you can confide, reach out to a religious leader or a support group where you can express your feelings. Additionally, you may decide to find professional help, and you can read more about that in Chapter 11.

Maintain Normalcy

During times of difficulty, even small routines can give comfort to your family. Maintaining *normalcy* means trying to stay as close as you can to your established routines, rules, and limits despite a change in circumstances. If your family is displaced from its normal quarters at home or at school, then adapting your routines to the situation is necessary, and sticking to an adjusted schedule is helpful. Kids thrive on predictability because it gives them something to count on, so even in circumstances that blow life as they know it out of the water, having some semblance of the old routine gives them a familiar foothold as they navigate this new territory.

Within reason, your children need to know that keeping up with schoolwork is still important, that your expectations for behavior are still in place, and that if they cross your lines they will still be held responsible and negative consequences may result. While being sensitive to their hardship and flexible in your reactions, maintaining healthy and appropriate limits communicates to your children that life will go on despite the changes your family is undergoing at that moment.

During this difficult time, it's particularly wise to avoid the urge to overindulge your children. Whether due to guilt, pity, or shame, some parents let all routines and requirements for their children fall away. It may be tempting, because none of us likes to see our children suffer, and alleviating anything that we can control that causes pain or hardship may seem like the right thing to do. But this approach communicates only messages of fragility, incompetence, or doubt about their ability to get through this difficult situation. While kids may outwardly enjoy not having limits or rules, they'll pick up on these unconscious messages we send and internalize them.

You want to parent your children with the expectation that both they and you will come out of your current situation just fine—you'll all make it through together. You want to communicate messages of resilience, because you're not just parenting

Communicate messages of resilience, because you're parenting for the long run.

for this situation but for the long run. You will all come out of this and learn important lessons that will serve you well.

Let's take a closer look at some specific stressful situations.

Separation or Divorce

As difficult as separation or divorce is on parents, it can be even more difficult for children. A breakup is extremely stressful for all involved and there's no getting around that. However, you can set the stage for your children's longer term adjustment to this life event. Here are some tips for telling your children about a separation or divorce:

- Choose a public part of the home—*not* in their bedroom, which is often their safest place.
- Tell your children at the same time to maintain a sense of unity.
- Build in some time for them to prepare for the separation, but not so much that they can stew over it or start to think it won't happen.
- Try hard to keep your own emotions in check, even though this is easier said than done.
- Be direct and honest; don't hem-and-haw, trying to find a way to break it to them gently.

- Explain that it's not their fault. If they've recently been in trouble, you may need to call that out and make sure they don't connect the two events.
- Understand that even older children can be scared and blame themselves.
- Reassure your children that both parents will continue to love them.
- Answer any and all questions, even those that may seem to be inconsequential.

As difficult as breaking the news can be, managing your children's behavior during and after a separation or divorce can be extremely challenging. Of utmost importance is remaining on civil terms with your ex-spouse, because ongoing parental conflict following a divorce is one of the strongest predictors of negative outcomes for kids. This is emblematic of the Universal Strategy of role-modeling good behavior to your child.

From your child's perspective, he now has to navigate your two separate lives and deal with new and uncomfortable circumstances. For example, if your child is expected to live primarily with and love Mom, but see Dad on weekends and love him as well, if each of you says horrible things about the other, your child is then caught in the middle of an impossible situation. That child is liable to be left feeling vulnerable and unstable in both homes, and this will affect his behavior, his emotions, his grades—everything.

Keep the limits and rules at each home as similar as possible, though they don't need to be exactly the same. Kids can get used to different rules at different places as long as they are consistent in each. Use the Universal Strategies of giving good directions and enforcing limits and rules at your own home and, if needed, use coaching to help your children adjust to the rules when they are with their other parent.

Further, don't take actions that undermine the other parent. If the other parent is actively undermining you, and you don't have a civil relationship where you can compromise, then just focus on your own home's stability and rules. Resist the urge to retaliate or complain to your children about the situation. You can be a good role model for behavior regardless of whether your ex-spouse is doing so.

It's important not to share with your children how distressed, frustrated, or depressed you are about the situation. These are feelings that you must deal with using your own support system. You can't expect your children to handle that burden. Don't grill your children about your ex-spouse and his or her activities, either.

Children need both parents in their lives whenever possible. It's important that your kids have regular contact with you both and that each of you faithfully be there when scheduled. Also, give your children privacy and space to freely interact with their other parent without feeling like you're monitoring them.

> *Children need both parents in their lives whenever possible.*

All of these tips for breaking the news of a separation or divorce, remaining on at least civil terms with your ex, and keeping rules and limits intact will help you avoid some behavioral problems. Unfortunately, it's usually not possible to completely escape negative reactions to the breakup of the family. For this reason, redouble your efforts at the Universal Strategy of cultivating a positive relationship with your child, which will underscore the security and solid foundation of this changed family unit.

Even though divorce can be difficult, children can make it through resiliently and can even thrive in homes where each parent is happier and potentially more fulfilled in their own personal life. If your family life has already become acrimonious, it's not too late to take steps to turn that around. It will take time, but it can be accomplished. An amicable relationship between divorced parties is best for all involved, but if that cannot be managed, civility and avoidance of conflict between the adults will foster the best outcomes for the children.

Long-Distance Parenting

Divorce or separation is not the only instance in which a parent may be far from his or her children. Other situations can include military deployment or frequent or extended business trips. Regardless of the circumstances, when one parent is away for a long period, the child and the entire family can feel a great deal of stress. Long-distance parenting is not an easy task and requires focus, energy, and a commitment to maintain an active role in your child's upbringing. In short, you have to work much harder on the Universal Strategy of cultivating a positive relationship. Here are some ways to do that:

- Maintain regular and predictable contact with your child. Be faithful to your promises for calls and visits in order to be a source of predictability and security.
- Keep up with day-to-day details of your child's life, such as homework assignments, grades, and extracurricular activities, and know teachers' and friends' names.
- Find a shared activity to facilitate bonding, despite the distance. This can include interest in a sport, hobby, or favorite TV show.

- Use technology such as online video chats and playing online games together, or simply email or text, to help your child feel grounded, knowing you're easily accessible.

If your children start to show symptoms of stress during a period in which you are parenting long distance, you may need to be innovative with online versions of the Universal Strategies of coaching or practice sessions. Start a video diary of your day to show your children what you do when you're not with them. Let them know you're thinking of them constantly; you might even try turning the tables and ask for their ideas to help *you* get through the day without *them*.

If you're the parent left at home, you may choose to reevaluate what types of behaviors you choose to ignore. While you can't ignore everything, consider giving the kids a bit of a break on behaviors that may be annoying to you but can be prioritized low in the scheme of things. Use the Universal Strategies of praise and positive reinforcement more often. As stated earlier, don't forgo negative consequences or punishments for behaviors out of guilt or pity; stay consistent and your children will be able to get back on track faster.

Illness

Whether the illness you're dealing with is of a parent or a child in the family, this type of situation is extraordinarily stressful and delicate to address. In this book, we cannot begin to encompass all the potential aspects of such a situation. However, we do want to share some important advice for maintaining your child's emotional health and good behavior during this time.

First and foremost, maintenance of normalcy, as discussed earlier in the chapter, is absolutely crucial in the face of a serious illness. It is also extraordinarily difficult. Choose a few areas where you believe you can keep things the way they were before the onset of the illness. Perhaps it's only dinnertime. If your family always ate dinner together at 6 P.M., then make every attempt to maintain your routine, even if you have to eat off hospital trays and delay your meal until the completion of nurse's rounds. Children's hospitals typically understand the importance of these kinds of routines and have special amenities that families can utilize. If you're in an adult hospital, speaking to the nurse or physician about your child's needs can garner you an ally.

Additionally, try to refrain from overprotecting your children. You'll need to find that delicate, age-appropriate balance between the harsh reality of the situation and what they can or should know. Overprotecting your children sends a message that they can't handle whatever they are facing. Kids can sense when something is going on, and if they don't get answers from you, they'll fill in the gaps in their knowledge with ideas that can be worse than the reality. While you may be deeply concerned about

> *Overprotecting your children sends a message that they can't handle whatever they are facing.*

their ability to handle a serious health problem—either their own health issue, or that of a sibling, or even in yourself or your spouse—you must answer their questions and convey you're confident they can handle it.

If one child is ill, it can be extremely confusing and difficult for his sibling as well. Once you're back home and the initial emergency has hopefully turned to recovery, you'll want to get back to normalcy as much as possible. When you have to relax standards for an ill child, it's not unusual for sibling rivalry, and even jealousy, to creep in. If the situation allows, stick to the previous way you'd implemented the Universal Strategy of enforcing limits and rules. Keep to your family's chore schedule, amended as necessary, and supplement any changes with help from the giving good directions Universal Strategy. One child may have fewer or less difficult chores to complete, but chores should still be assigned to all, according to their capability: "Yes, Kendall has a different chore, but everyone takes a part in making our family work, and all of these chores are important." Or, "Jamal may not be able to go outside and play right now, but that doesn't mean the TV is going to stay on all the time; let's pick out some new books today."

Maintaining normalcy also means continuing the fun stuff: outings as possible, jokes, favorite foods, and even planned vacations if you can manage it. If you're concerned about the safety or health aspects of any of these kinds of things, discuss them with your doctor or nurse, and ask for assistance in amending them appropriately so that they can still be enjoyed by your family without any health setbacks.

It can be extremely gratifying to both children and adults to take part in advocacy activities that further their understanding of the situation. If a family member is in the hospital due to a car accident, learning about traffic safety and taking part in helping prevent other tragedies can be therapeutic for all of you. Similarly, if one of you is facing a disease or other kind of health issue, taking part in a walk or fundraiser can give you a sense of making a difference on behalf of your family. Sometimes, just being able to *do something, anything*, can positively affect your mindset by giving a sense of purpose and a feeling of empowerment. Often, participation in these kinds of events will also introduce you to other families in similar situations as well as support groups that are available to help.

Particularly in the event of a serious or terminal illness of a parent or child, we recommend that your family seek professional help. You can read more about this in the next chapter, but a professional who has experience in these types of circumstances can provide guidance and advice specific to helping each member of your family cope.

Financial Problems

Financial burdens or uncertainty can place a great deal of strain on a family. Kids pick up on cues from their parents, so the emotions you have (either overtly or covertly) are the ones that they possibly have. This is likely a situation for which they have zero context, and it's very common to see stress manifest in the types of behavioral changes we outlined at the beginning of this chapter: recurring stomachaches, withdrawal or aggression, avoidance, or sleep problems.

You may need to double-down on the Universal Strategies of giving good directions and enforcing limits and rules. Pair both of those with specific praise and reinforcement for any positive behaviors you can find. Make sure you look often for opportunities to praise and reinforce the good things they do.

Remember especially the Universal Strategy of being a role model for your children, showing them how to handle life's stresses. It's important to speak with a calm voice and demeanor, letting

Look often for opportunities to praise and reinforce the good things they do.

your children know what you're going through to the extent that they need to know and can understand. Here are some tips for coping with life changes due to financial hardship:

- Reassure your kids that you're taking care of them and taking charge of the situation.
- Explain what any changes in standard of living will mean as it relates to their lives.
- Alleviate misinterpretations that can lead to stress by answering their questions truthfully and age appropriately.
- Some changes, such as moving, may be unavoidable, but try to keep other major life changes to a minimum during this time.
- Hold a family discussion to address finances. Allow your children to share their ideas of where to cut back on family spending.
- Spend family time together doing low-cost or no-cost activities. Visit parks, go bike riding, play board games at home, and so on. Staying active helps keep excessive worry and feelings of depression at bay.
- Talk about the silver linings and help your family see the opportunities of change, such as perhaps pursuing a new job or living in a different part of town or the country. At the same time, keep the role of money in perspective.

Moving to a New Home or School

While the reasons for moving your family to a new home can be either happy or sad, the ramifications for a child are often similar: new school, new neighborhood, and (seemingly) no friends. The most important action you can take as a parent is to recognize that this transition can be tough and give your child as many coping skills as possible. Some kids adapt without a problem; other kids take months to adapt. Some of that is temperament, some of it is the age, and some of it is the situation.

Here are tips for helping your children deal with a move and for potentially avoiding many problem behaviors:

- Prepare them as far in advance as you can.
- Build their self-esteem by letting them make some decisions about the move: which items they will take and which they will donate, what color to paint their new room, and so on.
- Provide opportunities for open communication. Ask open-ended questions that can't be answered with just a *yes* or *no*, such as, "What do you think about that?" and "How does that make you feel?"
- Use role-modeling to show them how to adapt, but also let your children know that you're a little nervous about the move, too. After all, you'll have to start out in an unfamiliar place and make new friends.
- Put them in charge of the GPS/map and have them teach you how to navigate through town. Allow them to seek out their favorite chain restaurant or involve them in the quest to find the best ice-cream shop in the new town. This reframes a stressful situation into one that's fun and exciting.

In the situation of moving, consider creating a new normal.

Many of the same Universal Strategies suggestions for other life changes—maintaining normalcy and a routine—apply here, as well, but in the situation of moving to an entirely new place you may want to consider creating a *new* normal. Perhaps some of your routines or rules are a bit outdated, but you stuck with them simply because they *were* routine.

This could be a perfect time to update these choices or even advance them because your children are a little older. If you do decide to update, make sure you use the strategies of giving good directions and coaching and perhaps even practice sessions with the new rules so that this new normal is as successful as possible from the start.

This is also an opportunity to break out of a shell by starting a new tradition or activity. Try to budget some extra time and funds to allow your kids the luxury of something special or trying more extracurricular events than they might usually (without overscheduling yourselves, of course).

Some children, especially those who may be introverted or extremely set in their ways, may continue to have a hard time adjusting to life in a new location. Watch for signs that the stress of the move is not abating, specifically symptoms like withdrawal, irritability, aggression, excessive sensitivity, changes in eating habits, changes in school performance, and general changes in behavior that persist. If your child exhibits these behaviors and he continues after the rest of the family has transitioned to this new normal, then it may be worthwhile to talk with a professional. A list of the types of professionals available is in Chapter 11.

New Baby

Toddlers are famous for thinking that the new baby is an interloper, an invader into their territory, but it's not uncommon for older children to react this way as well. For these children, the baby throws a wrench into things and makes the circumstances of their life and place in the family very different. Even though you and your spouse may be overjoyed at your new addition, try to remember a time when you were thrown off by change and then keep that experience in your mind when dealing with your child.

In addition to maintaining as much normalcy as you can, pay special attention to making sure your older child's emotional needs are met. Use the Universal Strategy of cultivating a positive relationship with your older child by making sure there's a balance of individual time with parents and family time. Safeguard the extracurricular activities she enjoys, even if it's hard for you to handle them with a newborn. Utilize your support network of family and friends to make this happen. When your child feels secure in your love, a certain amount of sibling rivalry or deep-rooted jealousy can be prevented.

Allow your child to vent and listen carefully to her frustrations.

Acknowledging and validating your older child's sometimes ambivalent feelings and being ready to discuss her frustrations can make all the difference in her attitude. Instead of saying, "You should love your baby brother. How can you say such mean things?" allow your child to vent and listen carefully to her frustrations. Sometimes, the simple act of being heard has a healing effect. "Yeah, babies are loud and smelly; they are a lot of hard work."

This also lets you hear the root of her feelings, part of which may stem from not having her own emotional needs met. When you understand her feelings, you'll then know the specific steps to take to make her feel more secure. Continuing to follow up with validation will help: "You're already a fantastic big sister, the baby smiles at you more than at anyone in the family."

It can smooth the transition for an older sibling to participate in the baby's care in a supervised manner. This offers many opportunities for the positive reinforcement of his role as the older one." Give very good directions and coach your older child through this, making sure to use plenty of praise. This can be an incredibly empowering experience for your child.

But be careful in making your older children responsible for the baby, even if they are physically able to hold or change diapers. If they aren't comfortable or interested in doing this, you may create some resentment, which can build up. Instead, talk about how older kids can do so many things that the baby won't be able to do for a long time, and then brainstorm together about all the awesome things they will be able to teach the baby in the next few years.

•••

When the stress of a change in life's circumstances hits your family, it's important to be the shelter in the storm for your children. Cover them during the hard rain, assess the damage after the storm, and then give them the tools to rebuild themselves and help them along the way. Allow them ways to see any silver linings in those storm clouds. Identify the symptoms and investigate the root cause of stress. Role-model how to handle it appropriately. Use and adapt all of our Universal Strategies to benefit your child and the entire family during difficulties such as those we've outlined in this chapter. The stress of a situation like any of these can be managed, and in some cases ameliorated, so that the long-term effects are that your children grow stronger and more resilient. When handled well, the experience can teach them a great deal, because there's one thing for sure: There will be other stressful circumstances that will come along later in their lives.

11

Find Professional Help for Your Family

*W*hen life throws you a curveball, sometimes you need professional guidance to help your family navigate. The curveball could be troubling behavior changes stemming from an event such as divorce, illness, or death, as discussed in the previous chapter. Or it may be less drastic changes, but unfamiliar or unusual nonetheless—such as your child's frustration stemming from a suspected learning difficulty, aggressive interactions with peers, or unprecedented withdrawal from friends and family. Remember, your children's emotions come through in their behavior. Whatever your family is facing, you may feel as if your child's behavioral issues have tossed you into the deep end of the pool and you aren't sure which way to swim. Whether it's temporary or long term, when you find yourself dealing with a challenging situation or a problem that is increasing in its severity, you might decide you need to seek professional help.

Deciding when to get help is subjective; we all have a different line in the sand as to what we can handle and when we feel we're out of our depth. Only you will know where that line might be for you, and your line and your partner's line may be far apart.

In the midst of a family catastrophe, it's obvious there will be big changes to which all members must adapt. In some situations, there may just be a slow drift as your family adjusts to increasing dysfunction without recognizing it. In yet other situations, difficulties may develop or become more prominent as your child gets older. Over months, or even years, you may be running out of ideas or feel like you're at your wit's end. You might need an outsider's perspective, which is where that support network we advocated for you in Chapter 10 comes into play. Having trusted family members, close friends, religious leaders, and others you can rely on is crucial in offering up perspectives on knowing when the situation you are in has crossed a line. Soliciting their thoughts, which may confirm or reject your gut feeling about the situation, should be helpful in deciding whether to consult a professional.

There is still somewhat of a stigma attached to mental health issues, as well as to needing parenting help. It's important to get past that stigma if you feel overwhelmed or unable to cope. Getting help is not a sign of weakness or failure. It's doing what's best for your child and your family.

In this chapter, we identify some of the providers available to you and your family in the event you need them, and offer a number of reasons why you might want to seek professional help. We also list ways in which the behavioral issues we've already covered—tantrums, homework, mealtime, bedtime, attitude, and special situation stressors—can rise to the level of needing assistance. Finally, we discuss some safety issues when it comes to behavioral problems.

Determine Whom to Turn to for Help

Regardless of your support network, your child's pediatrician or your family doctor is often your first line of defense. Since you are your child's best advocate, you need to speak up when you're unsure or concerned about a behavior, an issue, or a situation. We know you don't want to come across as needy, high maintenance, or incompetent, or feel like you're the only parent who isn't sure what to do when a child's behavior escalates, but believe us, your doctor has likely heard your question before. Asking for help doesn't mean you aren't a good or a capable parent. Remember, your children's behavior is their way of communicating emotion or feelings, but sometimes important information can be lost in the translation between their behavior and their feelings. Professionals often can serve as an interpreter and help you zero in on the root of your child's behavioral problem.

> *Asking for help doesn't mean you aren't a good or a capable parent.*

Your pediatrician or family doctor can be the main point-person to triage the situation and either handle it with you or direct you to an appropriate resource. This could include a referral to a specialist for an evaluation of the problem and possibly intervention.

1. An *evaluation* of a problem helps define what's going on with your child, offers an understanding of that problem, and provides direction for an intervention. Targets for an intervention

can be identified and prioritized within the larger scope of the child's and family's specific circumstances and resources.

2. An *intervention* addresses the specifics as to how to deal with the problem, which could involve anything from tutoring to therapy to medicine to a nutritionist/dietician. Within this phase there are some problems that can be fixed, but more chronic problems will need to be managed through compensation, skill building, and accommodation over the long term.

An evaluation and an intervention are two distinct phases of care and may involve seeing separate providers for each.

When selecting a provider, keep in mind that most professions require a license or special certification as a means of ensuring basic qualifications, and requirements vary by state. Be sure to do your homework to find the right licensed provider for the issue with which you are seeking help. Here's a quick reference to what some of the most commonly referred types of specialists do:

> *Do your homework to find the right licensed provider.*

- *Psychologist:* Typically possesses a Ph.D., Psy.D., or Ed.D. Psychologists study and evaluate mental processes and behavior and provide mental health assessments and interventions. There are numerous subspecialists within psychology, including a child clinical psychologist, who specializes in psychological adjustment and disorders of mental health; a neuropsychologist, who specializes in the relationship between the brain and cognition/behavior; and a health psychologist, who specializes in the relationship between a child's mental health and physical health conditions.

- *Psychiatrist:* An M.D. who specializes in the prevention, diagnosis, and treatment of mental disorders. Psychiatrists can prescribe medications, and many possess a subspecialty working with children and adolescents.
- *Social Worker:* Helps people cope with many problems in their everyday lives. Clinical social workers can diagnose and treat mental, behavioral, and emotional issues. Some social workers also provide case management to help with hardships such as financial difficulties.
- *Marriage and Family Therapist:* Treats couples and families experiencing difficulties with interpersonal relationships.
- *Counselor:* Provides intervention and sometimes assessment services to empower individuals, families, and groups in dealing with issues related to mental health and education, as well as behavioral challenges within both of those categories.

Other resources for you and your child are his school teacher, nurse, counselor, and principal. These professionals work with children and see your child on a regular basis, so their perspectives can be valuable. The special-education department at your child's school can also be a wealth of local information about issues ranging from learning problems and behavioral issues to mental health diagnosis and treatment. Additional resources may be available by contacting your insurance company; employee-assistance program at work; or your state, county, or city governments.

Whomever you see, it's important to feel that the person you choose is credible and that you can trust his or her opinion. Various professionals and even specialists within the same broad profession may have different ways of approaching issues, and you should ask questions to feel confident that you are approaching evaluation or treatment in a manner that makes sense to you. Assessment and treatment of childhood issues should not feel like a mystery—there is no magic to the diagnosis and treatment of child and family issues.

Assessment and treatment of childhood issues should not feel like a mystery.

If you're seeking parenting guidance, you should have some level of agreement with the behavioral and parenting approach that the professional typically uses. If you're seeking therapy for your child, the fit between the therapist and your child is very important to facilitate effective treatment. There are numerous characteristics that may make a difference or play a role in helping you select a provider to work with your child. These include:

- Qualifications, experience, specialist certifications
- Geographic convenience
- Financial considerations (cost, insurance coverage)
- Gender
- Age
- Religious orientation (if important to you)

Good therapy can be uncomfortable at times as issues are addressed and progress is made, so don't jump ship at the first mention that your child didn't like something this professional said or did. At the same time, the relationship is important, so if you or your child are having trouble making a comfortable connection with the therapist, discuss the issue with him (professionals typically don't take this personally!). In some cases, arrangements may have to be made to transition to another specialist.

How to Decide to Call a Professional

There are many reasons why you might decide to see a professional for your child, yourself, or your entire family. As stated in the beginning of this chapter, each person's line is going to be different, and it's sometimes hard to know if you've crossed it. One way can be to take stock of the ways this problem you are having has impacted or obstructed your family or your child's life. This can mean an interference with social relationships, cognitive or academic development, emotional wellbeing, behavioral competence, or even physical health. The greater amount of disruption from the normal track the child's life has taken until this point, the higher the stakes of your family situation and the more you should consider leaning on professional help.

Evaluating and determining treatment is the job of the professional you bring in, and not yourself as a parent. We're explaining this not only in order to demystify the process of mental health evaluation, but also to give you some clarity in determining whether a situation in your family crosses the line between coping at home and needing help to cope.

In Dr. Pete's pediatric neuropsychology practice, he's seen many parents who tell him they waited and waited to seek help. Whether these parents delayed due to a stigma of taking their child to a psychologist or because they thought the problem would resolve itself, most of them stated they wished they had sought help much earlier.

The bottom line is that if you feel your child's quality of life is being negatively impacted, call and see if you can get some help. You can call for your own peace of mind, to increase your confidence in the track you've taken thus far, and in order to reduce your stress, as well as for the health, wellbeing, and safety of your family.

Take Stock of Your Family's Stress

Sometimes it's hard to see how stressful a situation is when you're in the middle of it. Try to reflect on what your life's stressors are right now and how they have impacted the day-to-day activities of each member of your family. These can include issues in your child's behavior at this time, but also anything in your work or personal life that detracts from your ability to parent effectively right now:

_____

_____

_____

_____

_____

Have you drifted into routines that adjust to the stress, even if they take you away from life as normal?   **YES   NO**

If yes, in what ways?

_____

_____

_____

_____

_____

Do you feel like you're at your wit's end dealing with this problem?   **YES   NO**

If you end up deciding to see a professional, bring this list with you as it will inform your evaluation.

Here are some examples of services that professionals can provide for children having specific types of troubles:

- Testing and/or intervention for a learning problem, attention problem, developmental concerns
- Assessment and/or intervention for a mental health condition, such as depression or anxiety
- Evaluation and/or intervention for a behavior disorder
- Evaluation and/or intervention for social difficulties

The list of reasons why you might seek help is long. This list encompasses only a few common ones and certainly is not the totality of reasons parents might seek help for their child or family.

Here are a couple of real-life examples needing varying degrees of assistance:

1. Michael and Tonya were concerned that something was going on with their seven-year-old son, Elijah. All of a sudden he was acting out in school, becoming aggressive at recess, and refusing to do his homework. They were fielding notes from Elijah's teacher at least once or twice a week, and then the principal started calling. They were both pretty stressed about the situation, having never before dealt with behavioral issues of any magnitude.

Michael and Tonya went in for a parent conference with the teacher, principal, and a school guidance counselor. In checking back through the instances of problem behavior at school, they pinpointed an uptick focused on the block of time the class works on reading, and recess, which falls directly afterward. Armed with that knowledge, they had Elijah tested for a possible learning disability in reading.

After getting the results of the evaluation, Michael and Tonya were able to make a more informed decision and use the resources available to them to get targeted help for Elijah. Once he felt more comfortable in reading class, he was able to behave better and the instances of aggression on the playground decreased dramatically. When he got help from a tutor, Elijah went back to completing his homework without meltdowns.

2. Rico and Maribel's daughter, Giulia, found herself suddenly without a core group of friends when her social group changed suddenly in the middle of fifth grade. As middle school loomed, her parents were increasingly concerned that Giulia seemed depressed. At home, she moped and lost interest in many activities and started complaining of a headache every morning before school.

Rico and Maribel talked first to the school guidance counselor, who shared some of the same concerns and recommended a psychologist. The psychologist they saw was similarly concerned about depression, but said the diagnosis wasn't certain at this point given that Giulia seemed to be reacting to changes in her social group. She gave Rico and Maribel some specific actions they could take to provide their daughter with additional social opportunities.

Meantime, the school guidance counselor asked Giulia to show a girl who'd just moved to town around the school, allowing for a natural new friendship to form. Rico and Maribel were able to reach out to that girl's family and foster the growth of that friendship. Together, the girls joined a recreational volleyball league and made friends with several teammates. Giulia's parents capitalized on her love of art by signing her up for a weekend oil-painting class, where she received positive feedback and a boost to her confidence. Rico and Maribel kept vigilant for signs of social distress and even depression in Giulia and the psychologist stated the family is welcome to return for a session should something else come up.

If you read through the previous chapters about specific behavior problem spots but felt your own troubles went beyond what was reflected in the strategies or examples, you might want to consider calling a provider for help. Parents can educate themselves on all aspects of childhood development, employ every strategy correctly and fully, and still not solve the problem.

In some cases, you may need an outside perspective to see the problem clearly. In other cases, your child may need a professional evaluation and intervention. What follows are some of the problem areas that we've previously discussed and indicators that professional help may be needed:

- *Tantrums* that are intense and continuing at the same frequency even though you are using the right Universal Strategies, or habitual tantrums that involve destructive and/or violent behavior.
- *Homework-related issues* that have been the basis for a battle every night with the child hating school, refusing to do homework assignments, and grades declining.
- *Mealtime* problems when the child is so disruptive that the family literally can't have a meal.
- *Bedtime* problems when the child doesn't sleep, affecting his or her performance at school during the day and/or family members' sleep at night. (A common red flag is communication from a teacher about the child's problems staying alert or paying attention).
- *Attitude* behaviors that have turned into a battle of wills, with every interaction seeming negative, deeply affecting the parent–child relationship.
- *Social* issues if the child is experiencing peer neglect, and certainly if he is experiencing peer rejection, is being bullied, or has been accused of bullying.

- *Catastrophic* family stressors such as a terminal illness or death of a parent or sibling, as well as when there are signs of stress with a divorce or a move.

Recognize When a Behavior Is a Serious Concern

The safety of your child and your family is your first priority. Any time you feel as if a child's behavior presents a danger to himself or to others, you *must* reach out for help.

Keep in mind that in children of this age, behavior is their way of communicating emotion. They may not have all the words, or even the self-awareness, to explain that they are having a problem. Instead, they may act out, or withdraw, as a way of expressing

> *If a child's behavior presents a danger, reach out for help.*

their feelings. A *marked change* in behavior is often a key indicator of stress. Change doesn't always mean there's a problem, but it should be a red flag for you to consider what's going on around your child.

Examples of some of the behaviors that can be serious include the following:

- Talking about or attempting to harm self or others
- Aggressive, violent behavior
- Depressed or irritable mood
- Social withdrawal
- Feelings of worthlessness, hopelessness
- Anxiety, extreme fear or avoidance (of a person or place)
- Bullying or being targeted for negative interactions from a peer

When considering these behaviors, look, too, to your child's social media accounts if she is allowed access. Permitting your child to use social media is a parent's decision, but not something we advocate in the age range of 3 to 11 years old. Nonetheless, reviewing your child's activity history can allow you to spot a problem. In some cases, a child may be feeling worthless, anxious or violent or show other emotions we have discussed without taking concrete action on those feelings. However, she may test the waters by posting clues on her social media pages that she is having these feelings.

> *She may test the waters by posting clues on her social media pages.*

It is *critical* that parents who allow access to social media monitor their children's activities. For the child's safety, anything a child posts should be taken with the same degree of seriousness as if he had said it out loud. If it's innocuous, then you can teach him a hard lesson about appropriate posting. Otherwise, you may have caught something in its early stages and can take steps to address it immediately.

Don't take chances. If your child's behavior leads you to suspect there is something serious going on under the surface, contact your family doctor or other professional listed in this chapter and ask for help.

• • •

Deciding to seek professional guidance for your child or your family is not always easy, but it can be the best thing you've ever done to help them. Steer clear of the stigma of getting professional help by not buying into it and know that you are investing in your child's long-term emotional and physical health. Whether you seek assistance from a psychologist, psychiatrist, therapist, counselor, or other type of professional, your child, and indeed your entire family, can benefit.

12

Conclusion

Discipline is not an insurmountable challenge. From understanding how to decode your child's behavior using the ABCs—*Antecedent, Behavior, Consequence*—to filling up your parenting toolbox with our 16 Universal Strategies, you should now be able to deal with problem behavior in your child and lessen some of the stress you may have felt. Specific areas of difficulty, such as tantrums, homework, mealtime, bedtime, and attitude, should be easier to handle, and you can turn what once was problematic into a positive experience for both you and your child. It's our goal that you now feel more confident, assured of yourself, and knowledgeable about the reasons that the tips and tools in this book can work.

You can turn what once was problematic into a positive experience.

Make these strategies your own. They are aligned with the basic tenets of child development, so they're adaptable to your individual child and your specific family circumstances. Combine your answers to the reflective questions we posed in this book with our Universal Strategies and you'll have the best discipline plan for you. *You* are the expert on your own family.

Parenting is a process. There's no absolute right or wrong way to do something, and with our Universal Strategies you can tailor your strategies to your individual child and the specific situation in which you find yourself at any given moment. The Universal Strategies give you a framework for supporting your approach to your child. Don't feel guilty or buy into feelings of inadequacy about any of your parenting mistakes. We *all* make them.

Most important, throughout any parenting dilemma that comes your way, remember:

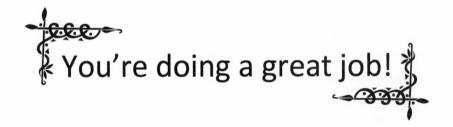

You're doing a great job!

Getting this peek inside your child's brain allows you to learn how it works. Knowing this, you can fix problems when they arise and prevent problems that might occur. The key to becoming and remaining stress-free is this knowledge. It fully informs your decision making and reactions and it allows you to be confident in your parenting skills. Confidence is crucial, so believe in yourself and in your child.

No parent, however, can fix or alleviate every problem. It's impossible. Besides, children learn through challenges and hardship. That's where they build resilience and character, as well as empathy for others. No child can learn to be resilient without the necessary opportunities. Allowing your child to get into situations where rejection or failure is a possible outcome is important to his or her development. Try not to be risk-avoidant for your children. Let them wander into the natural situations in which rejection or failure is a possible outcome and let them find their own way out. Allowing your child to fail is being a good parent.

> *Allowing your child to fail is being a good parent.*

Your children will push boundaries to see how much they stretch, test patience to see how far it can be pushed, and try out different mannerisms to see what will be acceptable. It's your job to let them know what's acceptable and what isn't in order to prepare them for membership in the social groups of friends, classmates, and teammates. Attitudes can push your buttons, but with this book you now have inside information on what's behind the eye-rolls, the sassy retorts, and even the lies.

If you're currently going through a major life transition, whether it's a new baby, a move to a new home, a divorce, a death, or financial troubles, you now have some insight as to how that can affect your children and steps you can take to help them through it. Maintaining normalcy, to the extent possible, will give them a familiar foothold as they navigate this new territory, allowing them some semblance of security and continuity of routine. Taking care of your own personal needs for physical and emotional wellbeing is crucial, and while it may feel selfish, it's actually the best thing you can do for your children. Here again, having confidence in yourself as a parent, and in your children's ability to overcome problems, will help you get through this difficult time.

If you feel you need to consider going to see a professional who deals with child behavior or mental health issues, we've given you some guidance on making that decision. Help is available through a family counselor, a school counselor, and family intervention programs, as well as through your pediatrician or your own doctor. Referrals to mental health specialists don't mean there's anything wrong with your child or your family; rather, it should be looked at as an additional resource made available to you. Seeing a professional can enhance your parenting techniques and does not replace them. If you feel as if a particular problem is negatively impacting your child's or your family's life, that may mean you've crossed the line and really should call in some help. This is especially crucial if you feel your child's safety, or that of any other member of your family, is in jeopardy due to a behavioral issue.

Gardening is an apt metaphor for parenting, since both necessitate the combination of thoughtful planning and preparation, as well as plenty of nurturing and guidance. Mother Nature also plays a role in terms of the number and magnitude of storms that pass overhead during the formative years. Ultimately, though, you're dealing with a living organism who has a different DNA than you, and so temperament, free will, and unpredictable reactions to stimuli can come into play.

Just as plants need feeding, watering, and monitoring on a regular schedule, you need to continue to use our Universal Strategies with your kids throughout their childhood, adapting

Continue to use our Universal Strategies with your kids throughout their childhood.

them as needed to the situations that arise. Before you know it, they'll blossom and grow under your guidance into strong, healthy, thriving, and beautiful individuals of whom you are immensely proud. And that's what *stress-free parenting* is all about.

• • •

Index